# THE ORIGINAL STORYTELLER

## Become a Better Storyteller in 30 Days

By Robert Carnes

"Story is powerful. It touches us deeply, in a way that's hard to explain. *The Original Storyteller* weaves an impressive array of stories, using examples from around the world and across the centuries, to showcase humanity's connectedness—and ultimately draw us closer to the writer of the greatest story ever told."

**Kevin D. Hendricks**
Editor, Church Marketing Sucks

"The church has the greatest story to tell, and we don't have to look far to learn how to tell it well. Robert reminds us to look for inspiration from the Original Storyteller. It's God's story, and He has given us everything we need to tell the world about Him."

**Justin Dean**
Co-Founder, That Church Conference

"With this 30-day devotional, Robert has created an intriguing union between personal spiritual development, pop culture, and Writing 101. Each day's entry flows and builds upon the previous day's reading with engaging, thought-provoking and entertaining insights.

"The way Robert unfolds God's storytelling methods inspires readers to create, imagine, and take action on their writing goals. *The Original Storyteller* is a motivating action plan for writers who want to discover how God uniquely creates and uses stories."

**Jennifer Wilder**
Digital Marketing Manager, The reThink Group

"Ever wonder the elusive formula to a compelling story? Read no farther than this inspiring, practical book. Great stories change everything—and this book will do the same for you."

**Mark MacDonald**
Strategic Communication Catalyst, Florida Baptist Convention
Best-Selling Author, *Be Known For Something*

"Through an undeniably entertaining and enlightening mash-up of English Lit, Film Studies, and Theology 101, *The Original Storyteller* inspires artists to reconnect their craft to their Creator. Robert has produced a true gift for anyone who feels stalled—creatively or spiritually."

**Kelley Hartnett**
Writer and speaker

"Storytelling is the most powerful form of human communication. *The Original Storyteller* allows you to immerse yourself in the form and function of story through bite-sized daily devotions."

**Brady Shearer**
CEO, Pro Church Tools

"From beginning to end, *The Original Storyteller* will leave you inspired and filled with a new appreciation for the art of storytelling. I love what Robert has done with the elements of each daily devotion. It's not simply a feel good story with scripture at the end. Each day gives the reader a chance to engage with scripture in a way that highlights the elements of storytelling, along with a prayer and action step to take. Get ready to dive deep into the scriptures and discover how to enhance your storytelling so you can tell the greatest story ever told."

**Rev. Meghan Howard**
Pastor, Fairborn United Methodist Church

"*The Original Storyteller* uses faith to communicate how God was the first Storyteller and that we can be empowered to do the same. It's a really unique approach to encouraging people to be creative in the way they tell stories. People who read this book will be inspired to be creative."

**Terence Lester**
Founder, Love Beyond Walls

"I encourage you to embark on a 30-day journey with Robert Carnes as he unveils stories from the viewpoint of God and how they connect with different narratives in making the work of God come alive. Robert ties a beautiful bow on each day's devotional by challenging you to think about an action that you could take on that day that would help you to author the story of your life. Read, be blessed and enjoy!"

**Dr. Ike Reighard**
Senior Pastor, Piedmont Church

"In *The Original Storyteller*, Robert offers a simple and very practical guide to the art of storytelling. You will be inspired and challenged as you work your way through this 30-day devotional that will ultimately help you bring out the best in your own story."

**David Clark**
Copywriter, James & Matthew

# DEDICATION

To my wife, Victoria
Our life together is my favorite story.

"Those who tell the stories rule the world."
**—Hopi Native American proverb**

"People think that stories are shaped by people.
In fact, it's the other way around."
**—Terry Pratchett**

# TABLE OF CONTENTS

# FOREWORD

As a child, stories were a huge part of my day. Each night, when my dad tucked me into bed, he'd tell me a story. He was a master at storytelling. They always involved some sort of crazy hijinks from his childhood.

He had one of those *Wonder Years*-type upbringings. Typical Midwest family. His dad was a WWII veteran with a past he'd rather not discuss, pushing him to a life of solitude at the junkyard where he worked.

His mom was an active member of the American Legion. And my dad was the ultimate picture of Americana. Blonde hair, blue eyes—a true Gerber baby all grown up.

My dad had crazy friends who always seemed to get injured in biking and sledding accidents. His first job was a paper route where, through somewhat genius and dubious techniques, he earned a free trip to Europe for his excellent sales numbers.

My dad had countless stories, filled with adventures and eccentric characters. I could never get enough of them. I even requested he retell some of my favorites.

Stories have a way of capturing our imaginations. Whether you're a kid or a full-grown adult, stories bypass your critical nature and go straight to the heart. There's nothing else that so easily grabs our attention and makes us listen.

But the most important part of the stories my dad told me was the fact that I got to know him. His stories revealed his heart to me. They revealed tiny glimpses of who he is.

Forgive the imperfect example, but the Bible is God's bedtime story for us. Yes, there are crazy antics and fascinating characters.

But the stories reveal the heart of the storyteller—the heart of our God. He tells, we listen, and we learn more than just the facts of the story. We learn about God.

That's why I'm so excited my friend Robert put together this devotional about storytelling. We get to connect our stories to God's stories, and ultimately, hearts connect to hearts.

As we learn to tell better stories by dissecting God's great narrative, we'll learn about ourselves, about our God, and how He can speak through us in fascinating ways.

Dig into these devotionals. Let them be your treasure map as you excavate the gold buried in the story of our Creator. You're in for an excellent journey.

**Jonathan Malm**
Author, *Created For More* and *Unwelcome*

# INTRODUCTION

O nce upon a time, there lived a king who discovered that his wife, the queen, was being unfaithful. Enraged, he had her executed and decided that no woman could be trusted. The king began marrying a new woman every day. The day after her wedding, each new queen would be beheaded before she had a chance to dishonor the king.

Not surprisingly, it became difficult to find women willing to marry the lunatic monarch. The king's chief advisor was tasked with finding suitable brides. The king threatened to kill the advisor unless he produced another wife.

To save her father, the chief advisor's daughter volunteered herself as the next doomed queen. The advisor begged his daughter not to do so. He would rather die in her place. But she insisted. She told her father that no more innocent women should have to die because of their homicidal ruler. With no other option, the advisor relented.

So the chief advisor's daughter married the king. On their wedding night, the queen offered to tell her new husband a story. He agreed, knowing that she'd be killed the next morning regardless. He might as well grant her last wish.

The queen told a beautiful story that lasted the entire night. Right as the story reached its climax, dawn broke. The queen stopped the tale. She acknowledged that the time of her death had arrived. Upset, the king demanded that she finish the story.

The queen agreed to finish the story only if he allowed her to live another day. The king reluctantly agreed. The next evening, the queen finished her first story. Immediately, she began a second story, even better than the first.

In the same fashion, the story was interrupted just as the next morning arrived. Again, the king commanded that he hear the story's conclusion. Again, the queen insisted that she be permitted to live another day.

This cycle repeated in the same way for one thousand and one nights. Each night ended with a cliffhanger and the promise of one more day's life. Through her stories, the queen gradually convinced the king to keep her alive permanently.

The king finally saw reason and ceased with his threats of death. The entire kingdom breathed a collective sigh of relief. And they all lived happily ever after.

This is the frame story for *One Thousand and One Nights*, or, as it's sometimes called, *The Arabian Nights*. The stories told by Queen Scheherazade to her maniacal husband are the stuff of legend. These include the stories of *Aladdin and the Magic Lamp, Ali Baba and the Forty Thieves,* and *Sinbad the Sailor*.

These tales also show the power of stories. How else could Scheherazade have convinced the crazy king to keep her alive for another day if not for the promise of another compelling story?

Stories are everywhere. They are the common theme shared by all people. They exist in every language, culture, time period and nation. Stories engage and entertain. They create emotion and empathy. Stories unite and connect.

But why? What makes stories so powerful? Why are they so universal? How is a good story able to penetrate the distractions of a busy world? What causes a story to activate the minds of people anywhere?

There are many reasonable explanations involving biology and psychology. Essentially, the human brain is wired to the storytelling frequency. Telling stories is a way to engage our minds on the most primitive level. They resonate down to our core.

That explains the how, but not the why. The science shows a connection between our minds and the stories we tell. However, this connection is more than mere coincidence.

We're attuned to great stories because that's exactly how our heavenly Father made us. The Bible says that we were made in His image. And that same Bible demonstrates that God is a master narrator. He's the Original Storyteller.

The Bible is one massive story. It's the story of the creation of the Earth, the birth of mankind, our original sin and the redemption through Jesus. It's the story of us and God and our ever-changing relationship.

There's a reason the Bible is the best-selling book of all time—it's the Greatest Story Ever Told. And God is the Greatest Storyteller.

As storytellers, we can use the lessons and examples of scripture to tell better stories. The principles of great stories are found throughout the Bible. The fingerprints of these biblical stories are embedded in the narratives mankind has told for centuries. It's woven into the fabric of our culture and behavior.

Let's explore some of those lessons together. Let's discover what makes stories so important. And learn why God is the Original Storyteller.

# HOW TO USE THIS DEVOTIONAL

## THE BIG IDEA

These are short summaries of the concepts presented each day. Think of them as quotable snippets of what's being presented. Check out the back of the book for a full listing of all these ideas.

## SCRIPTURE

Each day has a collection of Bible verses that corresponds with the devotional text. These scriptures are specifically pulled from the New International Version translation of the Bible.

## DEVOTIONAL READING

The daily reading is the meat and potatoes of the devotional. Each reading begins with a story—they're from a mix of books, movies, theater or real world narratives. The story provides an example of that day's principle and shows how it relates to God's story.

## PRAYER

What good is talking about God if we don't bother talking to Him? Prayer is an opportunity to reflect on and process what you learned from the reading. The written prayers are meant to get you started.

## ACTION

What good is reading about storytelling without acting upon what you've learned? Every day has an action that allows you to put into practice the lessons from each devotional.

# WHO THIS DEVOTIONAL IS FOR

This devotional is written for everyone who loves a good story. It's for everyone who wants to learn how to tell better stories. It's for everyone who wants to know God better.

In short, it's for everyone.

Admittedly, this devotional is perhaps best suited for church leaders and Christian creatives. That's my background and the audience I know best. However, I've written the stories broadly enough to apply to nearly anyone.

# ONCE UPON A TIME...

Because that's just how good stories begin.

# DAY 1

# IN THE BEGINNING

**BIG IDEA:** A story's beginning sets the tone for everything that's about to happen.

> In the beginning, God created the heavens and the earth. Now the earth was formless and empty, darkness was over the surface of the deep, and the Spirit of God was hovering over the waters. And God said, "Let there be light," and there was light.
>
> God saw that the light was good, and He separated the light from the darkness. God called the light "day," and the darkness He called "night." And there was evening, and there was morning—the first day. —**Genesis 1:1-2**

In 1830, Edward George Bulwer-Lytton wrote the novel *Paul Clifford*. Almost 200 years later, the book is largely unknown, except for its opening sentence:

> It was a dark and stormy night; the rain fell in torrents— except at occasional intervals, when it was checked by a violent gust of wind which swept up the streets (for it is in London that our scene lies), rattling along the house- tops, and fiercely agitating the scanty flame of the lamps that struggled against the darkness.[1]

Critics point to this opening line as the worst introduction to any novel ever. The sentence is long-winded, uninspiring, confusing and rambling. It's so hilariously bad, there's even an annual writing contest in its (dis)honor called the Bulwer-Lytton Fiction Contest.[2]

---

1   Lytton, Edward Bulwer Lytton. Paul Clifford. London: H. Colburn and R. Bentley, 1830.
2   www.bulwer-lytton.com

If *Paul Clifford* gives us an example of a terrible beginning, then the Bible serves as its contrast. Read the first sentence from the book of Genesis; you may even have it memorized. It's that simple, impactful and memorable.

> In the beginning, God created the heavens and the earth.

In ten words, this sentence sums up the entire first chapter of Genesis. That's the power of a good beginning and the essence of effective storytelling. Always begin by drawing in the audience.

Almost every story begins *in medias res*—a Latin term meaning "in the middle." This is because almost all stories have something that comes before. The opening line places us in the midst of a situation that will be explained during the course of the story.

The exceptions to this rule are creation myths. Every culture and religion has some explanation for how the world started. And nothing comes before the beginning of the world.

These traditional stories helped ancient societies make sense of their world. These historic peoples understood the importance of story in helping explain the unknown.

A common theme in these myths is an all-powerful being who establishes the world from nothingness and creates order from chaos. It's not a coincidence that folklore from across the globe shares so much in common with the biblical creation.

That's because each of these stories shares an origin in the same true story. God's creation of the Heaven and Earth had an influence on every part of mankind. This impact came even before the story was recorded in the scriptures.

The beginning of the Bible is *the* beginning. The Bible's origins come from the creator Himself. No one and nothing was around to witness the Earth's opening act except for Him. Our heavenly Father tells the story of how He shaped the Universe from nothing.

Genesis[1] sets the stage for the rest of the biblical story. This first book introduces several themes, including sin, redemption and man's relationship with our Creator. These motifs play an important role within God's narrative.

Memorable beginnings are crucial for any meaningful story. A story's opening should draw in the reader, while making promises about what to expect later on. Without a good start, even the best stories fail to launch.

## PRAYER

God, thank You for starting off the story of life with an amazing beginning. Your creation of the world sets the stage for the Greatest Story Ever Told—Your story.

It's hard to believe that we can have a personal relationship with the Creator of the Universe. Help us to better understand the importance of this beginning. Show us how it plays into our lives and the stories we tell. Amen.

## ACTION

Write the first sentence to a story. Make something up off the top of your head. Don't think too much about it—jot anything down. Now imagine where the story could go from there. What tone does this opening line set? What kind of story is beginning to form already?

Write two more opening sentences for fun. How are these two different from your first? What kind of stories would each of these sentences lead to? Let these beginnings get the creative juices flowing.

---

1   Which means *beginning* in Greek.

# NOTES

# DAY 2

# CREATED TO CREATE

**BIG IDEA:** Storytelling is part of our DNA because we were modeled after the Original Storyteller—God.

> So God created mankind in His own image, in the image of God He created them; male and female He created them. —**Genesis 1:27**

> For we are God's handiwork, created in Christ Jesus to do good works, which God prepared in advance for us to do. —**Ephesians 2:10**

Homer's *Odyssey* is one of the greatest epic poems ever told. It's the story of the Greek hero Odysseus and his ten-year journey home after winning the Trojan War. First told in the 8th century, Odysseus' challenging quest has greatly influenced Western storytelling.

In the poem's first lines, Homer calls to the mythological muses to sing Odysseus' story through him. The legendary blind bard did not take credit for the epic tale. Rather, he attributes the story to a higher power.

> Sing in me, Muse, and through me tell the story
> of that man skilled in all ways of contending,
> the wanderer, harried for years on end,
> after he plundered the stronghold
> on the proud height of Troy.[1]

The ancient Greeks believed that the Muses would descend upon mortals to aid in the creation of art. This is one of the earliest exam-

---
1 English translation by Robert Fitzgerald in 1961.

ples of divine inspiration. The concept of stories being influenced by a higher power is as old as storytelling itself.

These days, we have our own type of divine inspiration. But, ours comes from a different source—God, who is the Ultimate Storyteller. Although written by human hands, the Bible itself was shaped by God through man.

The Bible tells of God's creation, which is one big story. His desire to create and tell stories resides within each of us because He modeled us in His own image.

Each of us has a desire to create because God first created us. We were created to create—for from creation comes creativity.

This drive to create is one of the reasons stories play such a powerful role in our lives. We are compelled by our God-designed fabric to tell and hear stories. These narratives are expressed through the written and spoken word, acted on stage, sung in music and shaped into pieces of art.

There are hundreds of different forms of storytelling. Each of us tells stories in our own unique way. There is something about a good story that resonates with us to our very core.

A good story helps us recognize truths about ourselves and the world around us.

When God formed the earth, He filled it with the vital elements of any good story. These narratives have been playing out since the beginning of time. Many of the best stories are captured in the Bible. They get to the heart of what life is all about. These universal truths are why the Bible is still relevant after thousands of years.

When Jesus walked the earth, He often spoke in parables. These were earthly stories used to illustrate a heavenly message. Jesus knew that teaching in the form of a story would help people to better comprehend them.

These stories resonated with Christ's audience at the time because they were relevant. We can relate to their meaning even today. By using parables, Jesus embodied God's commitment to storytelling.

Stories are one of the ways we can see God at work in our world. Evidence of His creation is all around us. Our love of stories was placed in our hearts by our heavenly Father.

As each of us is a part of God's creation, we also play a role in His never-ending story.

## PRAYER

God, thank You for making us in Your own image. Thank You for giving us the ability to create and appreciate stories of our own. We are driven by the same desire for story that You instilled within us from the beginning of time.

Help us use this storytelling instinct to discover truths about ourselves and about you. Help us to listen to the stories of others and understand that all stories originate with You. Amen.

## ACTION

Where do your ideas for stories come from? What motivates you to tell stories? Write down at least three inspirational sources for your storytelling. This can be everything from a quirky neighbor, tales from your childhood or an especially vivid dream.

Understanding your inspirations helps you better harness and focus these creative energies. Tap into your storytelling instincts. Figure out where they come from and where they might lead you.

# NOTES

# WORDS

**BIG IDEA:** Words are the basic building blocks of every story.

> In the beginning was the Word, and the Word was with God, and the Word was God. He was with God in the beginning. Through Him all things were made; without Him nothing was made that has been made. In Him was life, and that life was the light of all mankind. The light shines in the darkness, and the darkness has not overcome it. —**John 1:1-5**

A li Baba was a poor woodcutter, whose greedy older brother, Cassim, was a wealthy merchant. One day as Ali Baba was gathering wood, he witnessed a band of forty thieves approaching a cave. They stopped and spoke the words:

"Open sesame."

The cave magically opened to reveal a hiding place for the thieves' treasure. Once they deposited their loot, the thieves sealed the doors shut with another set of magic words:

"Close sesame."

Intrigued, Ali Baba waited until the thieves left. Then, he snuck into the cave using the magic word. He took a single bag of gold, hoping that this treasure would give he and his wife a better life. More importantly, he hoped that its disappearance would go unnoticed by the thieves.

It wasn't long until his older brother, Cassim, learned of the cave and the treasure. The greedy brother forced Ali Baba to reveal the secret location. Cassim immediately marched to the cave and spoke the magic words. The cave opened to allow Cassim entrance. Then, the doors closed behind him.

The greedy man began to steal as much gold as he could. In his excitement, he forgot the magic words to exit the cave. Cassim was trapped until the forty thieves returned and killed him for attempting to steal their gold.

*Ali Baba and the Forty Thieves* is not the only story to demonstrate the power of words. Countless fictional wizards and witches use magic words to derive their powers. Spies and secret agents use code words to aid in their espionage. Some superheroes, like Captain Marvel, even use magic words to transform into their super selves.

Words are a key that open doors to new worlds and new opportunities. Words contain knowledge and knowledge is power.

There is a reason that the Bible says God spoke the world into being. There's also a reason that the Jewish name for God, Yahweh, means "He who speaks." In fact, the very name Yahweh became a sacred and unspeakable word in ancient Jewish culture. The word has power.

God used words to speak and write the world into existence. Jesus is the Word made flesh, sent to save us from our sins. God put His words on paper in the form of the Bible to provide daily instruction and insight.

Words should be important to us because words are important to God. Throughout history, God has used words to guide us and shape the way the world works.

Words represent ideas and express emotions. Words can lift people up or tear them down. Words can speak the truth or spread lies. Words can inform or persuade. Words can incite joy or sadness or anger or fear. The power to use words in these ways comes directly from God.

It's no wonder why words are also the building blocks of story. Think of words as actual building materials and a story as the finished product. Storytellers are wordsmiths; words are our raw materials.

Writing is as simple and as complicated as placing one word after another. Navigating the infinite choices of what word to use next can be overwhelming. There never seems to be a wrong or right choice. But, each word choice can make a major impact on a story.

Being a storyteller means selecting words and assembling them in a specific order to form a narrative. Choose your words carefully.

## PRAYER

God, thank You for giving us the words to communicate with You and each other. Thank You for speaking into our lives in a way that we can understand.

Help us to better understand the power of our words. Help us to always us them to Your glory and the improvement of our world. Show us the impact of the words we use and give us the insight to always use the right words for the right reasons. Amen.

## ACTION

Choose five of your favorite words. Write them down. Why do you like these words? What does each of them mean? What makes them stand out to you?

Now try and use your five words in a sentence. Can you arrange the words in a way that makes sense? Remember that all words have a distinct purpose, like each of us.

# NOTES

# DAY 4

# NARRATIVE

**BIG IDEA:** Narratives connect the elements of storytelling together into a recognizable pattern.

> This is the account of the heavens and the earth when they were created, when the Lord God made the earth and the heavens. —**Genesis 2:4**

> My people, hear my teaching; listen to the words of my mouth. I will open my mouth with a parable; I will utter hidden things, things from of old—things we have heard and known, things our ancestors have told us. We will not hide them from their descendants; we will tell the next generation. —**Psalms 78:1-4**

According to legend, Ernest Hemingway once made a wager with some friends. They bet $10 that the author couldn't write a complete story in only six words. Hemingway's work is renowned for its plain and sparing use of language.

But being limited to six words would be a real challenge. The Nobel laureate thought for a moment, wrote the following on a napkin and won the bet:

For sale: baby shoes, never worn.[1]

It's unsubstantiated if Hemingway's bet actually happened.[2] But it does prove one thing—a complete story can be written in only six words. Despite its length, this very short story still has a basic narrative structure.

---

1   https://en.wikipedia.org/wiki/For_sale:_baby_shoes,_never_worn
2   Snopes claims to debunk the story (www.snopes.com/language/literary/babyshoes.asp). But that's a story for another time.

Hemingway's six-word story has a beginning (For sale), a middle (baby shoes) and an ending (never worn). These six words are able to generate both the conflict and emotion needed to drive any good story. There is no word minimum for a story—the only requirement is narrative.

Narrative is often used as a synonym for story. But a narrative also gives a story structure. It's the connection between characters and events that gives a story definition.

Anything has the potential to be a story, but a narrative is what allows the story to take an identifiable shape.

Narrative and narrator both come from the Latin word *narrativus*, which means "to tell a story." In this way, we know that a narrative and narrator both supply the storytelling form. Both help us to see what the story contains and why it has meaning.

Although it's much longer than six words, the Bible also has a clear narrative structure. It contains a multitude of events that are all connected through the common theme of God.

It's an epic story that involves hundreds of characters and covers a wide period of human history. However, its narrative structure creates a cohesive story.

Stories have a beginning, middle and an end. These points are defined, even within the Bible. It starts with the creation of the Earth, deals with the fall and redemption of mankind and will end with the return of Jesus.

Even the stories within the Bible follow a similar structure. These stories interact and overlap with one another. But each has their own defined characters, setting and occurrences. Narratives are the skeletal structure that keeps the text from collapsing in on itself.

As a storyteller, always focus on that all important element of connectivity. Without some consistent theme or message, any story will unravel.

Understand what your story is trying to tell. Then focus everything else around that central point.

Stories take on a multitude of forms. But narrative is what distinguishes a story from random nonsense. Narrative gives stories clarity and purpose.

Without a compelling narrative, the story will languish and die—much like anyone listening to it[1].

## PRAYER

God, thank You for telling the story of the world. Thank You for giving this story a consistent narrative that includes You at the center. We've read about the beginning, live in the middle and know that You will be waiting for us at the end.

You are the great Narrator who shows us the true definition and meaning for every story. Thank you for making the narrative about Your love for us and Christ's death for our redemption. Amen.

## ACTION

Telling a story in six words is tough and takes some practice. It's easier to write a short story using only three sentences. Try writing one sentence for a beginning, another for the middle and the third for the end.

With three sentences, you should be able to create a narrative flow that leads your readers on a journey. Don't mistake narrative for a simple plot. It's deeper than the external events. Narrative is the internal connection that unifies these separate events.

---

1   OK, that might be overly dramatic.

# NOTES

# DAY 5

# PROTAGONIST

**BIG IDEA**: A protagonist gives personality and focus to your story.

> When the angels had left them and gone into heaven, the shepherds said to one another, "Let's go to Bethlehem and see this thing that has happened, which the Lord has told us about." So they hurried off and found Mary and Joseph, and the baby, who was lying in the manger.
>
> When they had seen him, they spread the word concerning what had been told them about this child, and all who heard it were amazed at what the shepherds said to them.
>
> But Mary treasured up all these things and pondered them in her heart. The shepherds returned, glorifying and praising God for all the things they had heard and seen, which were just as they had been told.
>
> On the eighth day, when it was time to circumcise the child, He was named Jesus, the name the angel had given Him before He was conceived." —**Luke 2:15-21**

A sailor named Marlow narrates Joseph Conrad's classic novel *Heart of Darkness*. In the book, Marlow captains a boat up the Congo River, into the heart of Africa.

Along the journey, the boat's crew hears rumors of an ivory trader named Mr. Kurtz.

Although he doesn't appear until the end of the story, Kurtz's presence is the main driving force for the other characters. Much of the book builds up to Kurtz's introduction. He is referenced often and characterized without being present.

Kurtz is someone who operates outside of the law. In the African wild, He gained a cult following based on his renown. The natives worship him like a demi-god.

Despite this, Kurtz dies of jungle fever shortly after the narrator finds him. Most of Kurtz's influence lives on through legends told by others.

Most protagonists are introduced closer to the beginning of the story. Kurtz is a rare exception. Another uncommon example of a protagonist's delayed introduction is Jesus. He is the long-awaited Messiah, the Savior of Mankind, the King of Kings.

For this reason, Kurtz is an example of a Christ-like figure. Conrad likely developed Kurtz using Jesus as inspiration. And he's not alone.

Think about any main character called a Chosen One or the answer to a prophesy. Everyone from Harry Potter to Neo in *The Matrix* owes their origin to Christ.

The Bible has plenty of major characters—Adam, Moses, Noah, Abraham, David and Joseph, to name a few. But there is protagonist that all these people were pointing to—Jesus.

That's how you can determine the true protagonist of any story. The entire narrative hinges on the influence of that character.

No story is complete without a protagonist—a more formal term for the main character. Compelling characters are what allow us to relate to a narrative. A strong main character provides a focal point for the story.

Without Jesus, the Bible is incomplete. Without His death and resurrection, the entire biblical narrative is meaningless. Jesus' life and sacrifice is what the entire rest of the story is building up to. His existence gives the story purpose.

# PRAYER

God, thank You for making Jesus the main character of Your eternal story. His perfect life serves as a great example for us to follow. His character is one we can all strive to emulate.

Although Christ only appears in the New Testament of the Bible, we still have the benefit of knowing how His character impacts your narrative. Thank You for focusing Your story on Christ so we can focus our lives on Him, too. Amen.

# ACTION

Write down a list of your five favorite protagonists. What characteristics make them memorable? What impact do they have on the narratives? Here's a list of some prime protagonist examples:

- Sherlock Holmes
- Dorothy Gale
- James Bond
- Luke Skywalker
- Ellen Ripley
- Hercule Poirot
- Daenerys Targaryen

Can you match each of these protagonists to the stories they inhabit? Odds are, they'll be just as memorable as the characters themselves. Because great characters make for great stories. And a strong protagonist is a driving force in making a story memorable.

# NOTES

# DAY 6

# SUPPORTING CHARACTERS

**BIG IDEA**: Effective supporting characters complement and amplify the actions of the story's protagonist.

> As Jesus was walking beside the Sea of Galilee, He saw two brothers, Simon called Peter and his brother Andrew. They were casting a net into the lake, for they were fishermen. "Come, follow me," Jesus said, "and I will send you out to fish for people." At once they left their nets and followed him. —**Matthew 4:18-20**

Frodo Baggins inherited the worst gift ever from his uncle Bilbo—the One Ring of Mordor. To destroy it, he must travel to an evil volcano hundreds of miles away. But he doesn't want to travel alone.

So Frodo invites his gardener, Samwise Gamgee, to join him on the journey. Sam is a typical hobbit, which means he hates adventures. He accompanies Frodo anyway.

And it's a good thing he did. Because along the journey, Sam becomes one of the most significant supporting characters in literature.

Carrying the One Ring was a heavy burden, like that of the cross. Through the *Lord of the Rings* trilogy, Frodo grows weaker as a result of the parasitic ring. He would have never made it to the end of the journey without a resilient and loyal companion.

When the rest of the Fellowship of the Ring splits, Sam insisted on continuing to go with Frodo to Mordor. When Frodo was captured by orcs, Sam took the One Ring himself and rescued Frodo. He was loyal and unfailing in the support of his friend.

When He was ready to begin His ministry, Jesus knew that He couldn't do it alone. Strolling beside the Sea of Galilee, Jesus spotted brothers Simon and Andrew fishing.

He told them to follow Him so that they might become fishers of men. Without hesitation, the two brothers dropped their nets and ran to catch up with the Son of God.

Jesus recruited the rest of the 12 apostles in much the same way. These were all average men, with no great wealth or social standing.

Yet, these were the men He selected as the foundation to start the early church. He handpicked His supporting cast because He knew how important they would be in God's story.

During Jesus' life, the apostles could be serious knuckleheads. They often missed the point of Christ's parables. They squabbled with each other over Jesus' favor. One denied Christ three times before His crucifixion. Another betrayed Jesus.

Their behavior demonstrates one of the key roles to supporting characters—providing context to the protagonist. The disciples' shortsightedness only serves to amplify Jesus' perfection. Where the disciples were human, He was divine.

After Jesus' resurrection, these apostles proved their true worth. They started the early church, defied oppression and became martyrs in the name of God. Showing their faith in Jesus was enough for them to overcome many challenges.

The apostles' accomplishments further showed the influence of Christ. Only through His guidance could these men exceed their limitations. Only Jesus could take a group of imperfect men and start an unstoppable movement.

That's what supporting characters do—they put the protagonist into perspective. They give us another reference point to which we can relate.

It's not always easy to live up to the perfection of Christ. It's easier to understand the struggles of a doubting Thomas or a willful Peter. These men show us how we can relate to Christ by how they related to Him.

Supporting characters are crucial to a story because they give depth to the narrative. They provide real examples for a protagonist to interact with and grow through.

Jesus is the main character of the Bible, but His story is magnified because of those people around Him.

## PRAYER

God, thank You for including real men and women in the Bible, like the 12 apostles. These flawed and authentic characters help us to relate to your story.

Through them, we better understand the character of Christ. Help us to see that we are also supporting characters in Your on-going story. Help us to know our roles and to use them to amplify Jesus' work. Amen.

## ACTION

What if you had a sidekick? Who would it be? Write a description of the ideal supporting character for the story of your life.

Invent some details about their background and the nature of your relationship. How does this sidekick impact your story? What does their description tell you about yourself?

# NOTES

# DAY 7

# ANTAGONIST

**BIG IDEA**: Antagonists stand in the way of the protagonist, driving conflict in the story.

> One day the angels came to present themselves before the Lord, and Satan also came with them. The Lord said to Satan, "Where have you come from?" Satan answered the Lord, "From roaming throughout the earth, going back and forth on it. —**Job 1:6-7**

> And the great dragon was thrown down, that ancient serpent, who is called the devil and Satan, the deceiver of the whole world—he was thrown down to the earth, and his angels were thrown down with him. —**Revelation 12:9**

There was once an angel considered the most beautiful in Heaven. He was a shining light and called the morning star. His name meant "bringer of dawn." This singular angel was charismatic, cunning and mighty.

Lucifer was also jealous of God's glory. He argued that God was a tyrant and that the other angels should share in ruling Heaven. He persuaded a third of his fellow angels to join him in a rebellion against God.

When this revolt failed, Lucifer rallied the fallen angels to follow him into Hell. There, he established his rule under the name Satan. As he laments in John Milton's *Paradise Lost*:

> It's better to reign in Hell than serve in Heaven.[1]

---

1    Milton, John. *Paradise Lost*. 1667. Book 1. Lines 258-63.

Satan makes many appearances in stories. He's in everything from Marlowe's *Doctor Faustus* (the original story about making a deal with the devil) to the Rolling Stone's *Sympathy for the Devil* ("pleased to meet you…").

In the classic comedy *Animal House*, Donald Sutherland plays an English professor who addresses his class about *Paradise Lost*. The word *Satan* has been scrawled on the chalkboard behind him.

> Now, what can we say of John Milton's *Paradise Lost*? It's a long poem, written a long time ago, and I'm sure a lot of you have difficulty understanding exactly what Milton was trying to say.
>
> Certainly, we know that he was trying to describe the struggle between good and evil, right? Okay. The most intriguing character, as we all know from our reading, was… Satan. Now was Milton trying to tell us that being bad was more fun than being good?[1]

In many ways, our culture is fascinated by the devil. But we have to remember the role that he plays in the biblical story—that of the antagonist.

The role of any (in)decent arch-nemesis is to thwart the good guy. The antagonist is the opposite of the protagonist—a villain, an adversary, an enemy.

Not all antagonists are necessarily evil or a prototypical bad guy. (For example: Inspector Javert in *Les Miserables*. The man was just trying to do his job.) But their one consistent characteristic is to oppose the efforts of the protagonist.

They represent the other end of the duality of man. The relationship between the protagonist and the antagonist drives the story's conflict. Antagonist comes from Greek, meaning to "struggle against."

---

1   National Lampoon's Animal House. Universal 8, 1980.

Their explicit purpose in the story is to serve as an obstacle for the protagonist to overcome.

Satan is the ultimate antagonist—the Big Bad, to borrow a term from *Buffy the Vampire Slayer*. The devil makes only a few direct appearances in scripture. But he's always lurking in the background, trying to cause trouble. He tests Job's patience, tempts Jesus in the wilderness and rears his ugly head quite a few times in Revelation.

Lucifer's purposes contradict those of God. Where God expects humility, Satan embodies arrogance. Where God calls for honesty, Satan is the great deceiver. Where God demanded submission, Satan gathered an army and tried to conquer Heaven.

The biggest difference between the devil and any other storybook antagonists is that Satan is real. He plays a role in our lives whether we realize it or not. Thankfully, Satan falls victim to one common story trope—that evil eventually loses to good.

## PRAYER

God, thank You for saving us from the power of the devil. He works in direct opposition to everything good in the world, including in our own lives.

Help us to see his presence so that we may avoid falling into his trap. Thank You for the redeeming power of Jesus' love that helps us to overcome the evil in this world. Amen.

## ACTION

List the five most memorable antagonists from stories. What makes them so powerful? Why is their character so hateful?

Next to each antagonists' name, list the protagonist from the same story. How do these two characters oppose one another? The differences between these two characters will be the tension that drives the story's conflict.

# NOTES

# DAY 8

# CHARACTER DEVELOPMENT

**BIG IDEA**: Development within a story's characters gives them depth and authenticity.

> Meanwhile, Saul was still breathing out murderous threats against the Lord's disciples. He went to the high priest and asked him for letters to the synagogues in Damascus, so that if he found any there who belonged to the Way, whether men or women, he might take them as prisoners to Jerusalem.
>
> As he neared Damascus on his journey, suddenly a light from heaven flashed around him. He fell to the ground and heard a voice say to him, "Saul, Saul, why do you persecute me?" "Who are you, Lord?" Saul asked. "I am Jesus, whom you are persecuting," he replied. "Now get up and go into the city, and you will be told what you must do."
>
> The men traveling with Saul stood there speechless; they heard the sound but did not see anyone. Saul got up from the ground, but when he opened his eyes he could see nothing. So they led him by the hand into Damascus. For three days he was blind, and did not eat or drink anything. —**Acts 9:1-9**

Saul of Tarsus was a Roman citizen, well-educated and respected. He came from a good family and was being groomed to be a high priest of the Jewish faith. Saul came from a devout sect of Judaism and approached his faith with great zeal.

He had a great deal of potential.

Saul was also a significant antagonist to the early church. He spoke against Jesus' teaching. He broke up churches and condemned Christians to death. Saul's efforts worked in direct opposition to Jesus' ministry.

Saul's actions were motivated by his dedication to Judaism. He believed that Jesus' followers were heretics. In his mind, their mission contradicted God's. As a result, he focused his attention on silencing them. He saw himself as the hero of the story, a champion of the faith.

All that changed on the road to Damascus. Saul got word that Christianity had spread to Damascus, the capital of present-day Syria. Saul got permission from the High Priest to travel there and warn the Syrian synagogues. He would stop at nothing.

On the journey there, Saul and his party were struck by a bright light. From this shining brilliance, Jesus spoke to Saul. He asked why Saul was persecuting His people. Saul was dumbfounded—for the first time, he began to question his convictions.

The light blinded Saul for three days. His traveling companions guided him into Damascus. There, he was cared for by a Christian disciple named Ananias. By the time Saul's sight returned to him, his life would never be the same.

God changed Saul into Paul. He transformed Saul into one of the most righteous advocates of the early church. In an instant, Paul traversed one end of the spectrum to the other.

His mission had switched from ending Christianity to spreading it. He would die for the cause that he once sought to end. He was a completely different person.

God used Saul to show that He has the power to change the hearts and minds of people to do His will. God demonstrated His ability to grow character even in the harshest conditions. The same zeal that had been directed against Christianity had been turned into a vehicle to grow the early Church.

Change is a powerful element within a story. Characters who don't change are predictable and flat. They aren't very interesting. Dynamic and fully-fledged characters develop new traits or characteristics through the narrative.

Conflict within a story serves as a catalyst to bring about character development.

Character development is compelling because real people change. A character's maturation gives us something to relate to. We empathize with their struggles and triumphs. Internal growth is one of the building blocks that establishes good stories.

Saul is one of many characters who changes during the course of scripture. The story of his conversion and actions are one example of the power of biblical storytelling.

Even more individuals have the opportunity to change their character as a result of hearing these stories. Their personal narratives become a part of the larger story of God.

## PRAYER

God, thank You for our ability to grow as people. Help us to see the development of others in our lives and in scripture. Teach us to learn from these examples and grow into better people ourselves.

Thank You for transforming Saul from a villain into a hero so that we know that our lives can be changed through you. Show us how we can develop our own character daily to be more like that of Christ. Amen.

## ACTION

Think of another character who undergoes a significant change within a story. Write a brief description of the character at the beginning of the story. Then write another description of how they turned out in the end.

What changed? And why? Identify the point in the story that moved this person from point A to point B. Remember that characters need to grow and adjust to give them depth and believability. The more drastic the shift, the more impact it can have on the story.

# NOTES

....................................................................

....................................................................

....................................................................

....................................................................

....................................................................

....................................................................

....................................................................

....................................................................

....................................................................

....................................................................

....................................................................

....................................................................

....................................................................

....................................................................

....................................................................

# DAY 9

# CONFLICT

**BIG IDEA:** Every story begins and ends within the structure of conflict.

> Now Abel kept flocks, and Cain worked the soil. In the course of time Cain brought some of the fruits of the soil as an offering to the Lord. And Abel also brought an offering—fat portions from some of the firstborn of his flock.
>
> The Lord looked with favor on Abel and his offering, but on Cain and his offering He did not look with favor. So Cain was very angry, and his face was downcast.
>
> Then the Lord said to Cain, "Why are you angry? Why is your face downcast? If you do what is right, will you not be accepted? But if you do not do what is right, sin is crouching at your door; it desires to have you, but you must rule over it." Now Cain said to his brother Abel, "Let's go out to the field." While they were in the field, Cain attacked his brother Abel and killed him.
> **—Genesis 4:1-8**

During the civil rights movement, two prominent figures took two different approaches to promote social justice. Martin Luther King, Jr., espoused peaceful marches and boycotts. Malcolm X preferred a more violent approach.

Both men wanted the same thing, but took opposite paths to get there.

These opposing viewpoints for a common cause inspired two comic book legends. Martin Luther King, Jr. and Malcolm X inspired

Charles Xavier and Erik Lehnsherr; better known as Professor X and Magneto of *X-Men* fame.

Like his real-life counterpart, Professor X fought for peaceful coexistence between mutants and humans. Conversely, Magneto asserted the super-powered mutants as a dominant species. He chose to fight against any opposition.

*X-Men* creator Stan Lee spoke about this duality between the two opposing viewpoints:

> I did not think of Magneto as a bad guy. He was just trying to strike back at the people who were so bigoted and racist. He was trying to defend mutants, and because society was not treating them fairly, he decided to teach society a lesson. He was a danger of course, but I never thought of him as a villain.[1]

Even if he wasn't a "bad guy," Magneto was still a constant opponent to the "good guys," the *X-Men*. He was doing what he thought was right, which made his convictions even stronger. This difference in opinion generates the central conflict in the *X-Men* storyline. This conflict is what propels the action forward.

Conflict is storytelling fuel. Without conflict, there is no story. No one likes conflict in real life, but it's what gives a story a reason to be told. Conflict facilitates character development and moves the story along the narrative framework.

Simply put, a story begins when the conflict is introduced and ends once the conflict has been resolved. It defines the beginning and end points of a story. Stories are ultimately about conflict.

Conflicts can be both internal and external. The best stories usually have a mixture of both. Characters' reactions to external conflicts usually reveal a deeper, internal struggle. Conflict is often the catalyst to meaningful character developments.

---

1   Marvel Spotlight: Uncanny X-Men 500 Issues Celebration, pp. 5-7

The story of Cain and Abel is the second biblical example of conflict.[1] The external conflict between Cain and Abel was a physical struggle, ending with Abel's death. However, the internal was much more significant.

Cain felt a jealous anger toward his brother. God favored Abel, and Cain envied that preferential treatment. He coveted the relationship Abel had with God. His internal conflict led to an external conflict.

This template for conflict plays out again and again throughout the Bible. Mankind tries to rely on his own strength, but succumbs to sin. God insists that mankind trust Him instead.

The overarching conflict within the Bible is between our sinful nature and God's call for us to return to Him.

That's exactly why the Bible begins with the story of Original Sin in the garden of Eden. And why the Bible concludes with a future vision of Jesus' return and the eradication of sin from the world.

In the meantime, the conflict described in the Bible continues to play out in our lifetime.

## PRAYER

God, thank You for helping us to overcome the conflicts in our lives. Conflict is inevitable, but you use these challenges to grow and shape us, as conflict shapes a story.

Help us to see the good in all situations and become better people through bad times. Thank You for the opportunities that conflicts bring and the resolutions you offer. Amen.

## ACTION

Think of a conflict. This could be internal or external. Or it could manifest itself in both ways. Brainstorm a story built around this central conflict. How is the conflict be introduced? How would it be

---

1   The first was that mess with the snake and the apple.

resolved? How does it impact the characters within the story?

Remember that a conflict is the dynamic force within a story. Imagining the conflict first can sometimes help to clarify the other storytelling elements.

## NOTES

......................................................................................

......................................................................................

......................................................................................

......................................................................................

......................................................................................

......................................................................................

......................................................................................

......................................................................................

......................................................................................

......................................................................................

......................................................................................

......................................................................................

......................................................................................

......................................................................................

......................................................................................

......................................................................................

......................................................................................

# DAY 10

# ACTION

**BIG IDEA**: Actions are the result of characters responding to conflict.

> What good is it, my brothers and sisters, if someone claims to have faith but has no deeds? Can such faith save them? Suppose a brother or a sister is without clothes and daily food. If one of you says to them, "Go in peace; keep warm and well fed," but does nothing about their physical needs, what good is it?
>
> In the same way, faith by itself, if it is not accompanied by action, is dead. But someone will say, "You have faith; I have deeds." Show me your faith without deeds, and I will show you my faith by my deeds. —**James 2:14-18**

A torrential rain causes a small town to flood. The citizens start to panic. But one gentleman remains calm in the face of the storm.

As the streets begin to fill with water, one woman paddles by in a canoe. She offers to give the man a ride. "Come with me and I'll get you to safety."

"No, thank you," he says. "I have faith that my God will save me." She shrugs and paddles away.

The storm continues to get worse. The rising waters force the man to retreat to the second floor. The first floor of his home is submerged.

A local family roars by in a speed boat. They notice the man looking out his second story window and draw closer. "Come with us," they call. "We'll get you out of here."

"No, thank you," he says. "I have faith that my God will save me." They shrug and speed away.

As the water overtakes the second floor of his home, the man climbs onto his roof. That's where the police helicopter spots him amidst the storm. "We're dropping down a ladder," a megaphone voice yells down to him. "Climb aboard. We'll rescue you."

"No, thank you," he says. "I have faith that my God will save me." The police in the chopper compel him to get on board, but he refuses—his faith is resolute. Finally, the helicopter leaves because of the storm.

The flood swallows up the roof and takes the man with it. In the strong currents, he is swept away and drowns. His spirit rises to Heaven where he meets God.

"Lord," says the man. "I remained faithful to you in the storm. Why did you not rescue me?"

"Are you kidding?" responds God. "I sent you a canoe, a speed boat and a helicopter. What more did you want?"

Stories are incomplete without the characters responding to conflict with action. These actions can be anything, so long as they matter to the characters and the audience. Story without action is meaningless.

Imagine if John McClane hadn't fought back when German terrorists took over the Nakatomi building in the movie *Die Hard*. What would have happened had Katniss Everdeen not volunteered herself for the Hunger Games? And the book of Exodus might have happened differently had Moses chosen to ignore that burning bush.

These stories would not have been possible without these characters' actions.

In the same way, faith without works is meaningless. We can't just sit around speaking or thinking about our faith. God compels us to act on it. The Book of James is famous for calling people out on this point.

The Book of Acts is an account of the actions taken by the disciples after the death and resurrection of Christ. Their response to His departure was to continue carrying out his ministry. They could have chosen to do nothing. Instead, they acted. Without their actions, the Church would not exist.

There's a reason a movie director shouts "Action" before rolling the camera. There's a reason the people in front of the camera are called actors. They're the ones who are carrying out the actions told within the story.

There's a reason that each day of this devotional has an action attached to it. It's one thing to read about storytelling, but to actually become a storyteller you must take action. These daily actions bring practical applications to each lesson. They allow you to work on improving your own stories.

Actions give a story life. And actions give our lives meaning. By acting, you can do something to progress both your story and your faith.

## PRAYER

God, thank You for giving us the ability to act on our faith. Without our actions, our faith would be just words and thoughts. Give us the courage and the motivation to live out our faith daily through our actions. Just as action moves a plot forward, so it does for our faith as well. May our actions advance Your kingdom on this Earth. Amen.

## ACTION

Jot down the first three action verbs that pop into your head. Now imagine a character from a story performing those actions. What happens? What are the implications of these actions?

Now write a paragraph describing these three scenes—one for each action verb. What's happening to the character both externally and internally as they perform these actions? Act these out yourself, if you dare, to get a visual example of the story.

# NOTES

# DAY 11

# DIALOGUE

**BIG IDEA**: Conversations build relationships between characters and give a story credibility.

> Let your conversation be always full of grace, seasoned with salt, so that you may know how to answer everyone.
> —**Colossians 4:6**

> In the past, God spoke to our ancestors through the prophets at many times and in various ways, but in these last days He has spoken to us by His Son, whom He appointed heir of all things, and through whom also He made the universe. —**Hebrews 1:1-2**

The year is 1941. The setting is a dairy farm in rural France. A troop of German SS soldiers descends on the farm house. Their leader requests to speak with the man of the house. They both sit at the kitchen table and begin a conversation.

This SS officer is quiet and pleasant. He is also nicknamed the Jew Hunter for his efficiency in tracking down "enemies of the state."

In calm and calculated words, the Jew Hunter reveals to the farmer that he is aware of the Jewish family hiding under the house's floorboards. The German officer speaks in English so the hiding family won't overhear their conversation.[1]

The farmer is given a difficult choice. If he confirms the Jews' hiding place, the German army will spare his family. Or he can resist, and the family will be discovered regardless.

---

1   And so that the American audience doesn't have to continue reading French subtitles.

48

Knowing he has no option, the French farmer tearfully consents. He points out where the family is hiding. Without dropping his smile, the German officer invites the rest of his troop in.

They proceed to fire machine guns through the floorboards. This kills all but one member of the Jewish family, a teenage girl, who is able to escape through a vent[1].

This is the opening scene to Quentin Tarantino's film *Inglourious Basterds*. It perfectly captures the director's signature style. Tarantino loves to blend lengthy, thoughtful dialogue with bouts of violent action.

This balance of witty conversations and brutal conflict are staples in films like *Pulp Fiction* and *Reservoir Dogs*. The fight scenes make the movies exciting. The imaginative dialogue makes the characters memorable.

Most of Tarantino's movie dialogue is not appropriate enough to reprint here. But rest assured, there's a lot of pontification to balance out the car chases and gunfights. When describing his signature style, Tarantio said:

> People tell me an interesting story in their life and I remember it. When I go and write my new characters, my pen is like an antenna, it gets that information, and all of a sudden these characters come out more or less fully formed. I don't write their dialogue, I get them talking to each other.[2]

Action is not enough to complete a story. In real life, people talk to one another. In a story, this is called dialogue. These are conversations between characters that contribute to the plot. Conversations are the storytelling equivalent of drawing people's hands in art—easy to do poorly, difficult to do realistically.

We all have conversations. It seems like writing them should be easy—but they're not. Many stories are propped up on unrealistic

---

1   Her life after that point is a whole different story.
2   "Quentin Tarantino." The Talks. The Talks, 24 Feb. 2017. Web.

dialogue. It's hard to make a conversation sound real when you're the one writing both ends.

Yet, dialogue is crucial to a story. It builds relationships between characters and creates a foundation for character development. Getting story conversations right takes time and practice. But is well worth the effort.

Like our lives, the Bible is full of conversations. But, the most important dialogue in scripture is between man and God. Our God reveals Himself by talking to us directly, or through prophets. Or burning bushes. Best of all, He invites us to join in a dialogue with Him anytime by engaging in prayer.

Jesus also had plenty of conversations with people. In many copies of the Bible, Jesus' words appear in red. That's because these are the words of God, spoken by His Son. These conversations stand out as significant. When Jesus speaks, we should listen.

The spoken word is important within any story. Getting dialogue right is a key step in establishing the impact of your story and personality of its characters. It doesn't always come easy, but when done correctly, it gives the story life and depth.

## PRAYER

God, thank You for speaking to us through prophets and Your son, Jesus. Help us to hear your words and understand their importance. Guide the conversations we have with others that we might develop better relationships.

Help these dialogues give us a better understanding of You and Your plan for our lives. Thank You for giving us the gift of conversation and the opportunity to speak to You through prayer. Amen.

## ACTION

Write a page-long conversation between two characters. It can be about anything—each other, the weather, the stock market or other riveting subjects. Try to develop the characters and their relationship through this dialogue.

Read the conversation out loud, either to yourself or with a friend. Does it sound like something people would actually say? Work on the words until they sound realistic. It will take a few tries to get it right. But creating convincing dialogue is crucial to storytelling.

## NOTES

...................................................................

...................................................................

...................................................................

...................................................................

...................................................................

...................................................................

...................................................................

...................................................................

...................................................................

...................................................................

...................................................................

...................................................................

...................................................................

# DAY 12

# POINT OF VIEW

**BIG IDEA**: Every story and every person has a unique perspective.

> All of us, then, who are mature should take such a view of things. And if on some point you think differently, that too God will make clear to you. —**Philippians 3:15**

> He determines the number of the stars and calls them each by name. Great is our Lord and mighty in power; His understanding has no limit. —**Psalm 147:4-5**

Wealthy British person Roger Ackroyd has been murdered. His fiancé was poisoned the night before. And that was after she was suspected of killing her former husband.

The situation is a bloody mess. Or the perfect recipe for a good murder mystery.

Enter famous detective Hercule Poirot to solve the complicated case. Assisting Poirot in his investigation is Dr. James Sheppard. Sheppard dined with Ackroyd the night of his murder and also narrates the story.

Most of the dinner party guest had alibis at the time of Ackroyd's murder. Poirot still suspects they are all hiding information. Several of them had a motive for murdering Ackroyd. The chief suspect in the investigation goes missing.

Amidst this chaos and confusion, Poirot assembles enough evidence[1] to identify the killer. The brilliant detective meets alone with Dr.

---

1  Using his famous "little gray cells," aka his brain.

Sheppard to reveal the murderer's identity.

Was it Ackroyd's niece who killed him? Or was it the housekeeper? Did the butler do it? As it turns out[1], it was the story's narrator, Dr. Sheppard, who killed Roger Ackroyd.

Agatha Christie shocked her readers with the twist to *The Murder of Roger Ackroyd* in 1926. The ending was so unlike that of any other mystery novel. Most mystery stories allow the audience to follow along and solve the crime with the detective through the lens of a trustworthy narrator.

Dr. Sheppard intentionally neglects to share key pieces of information. He deliberately leaves the audience in the dark. For that reason, he's considered an unreliable narrator. These characters tend to lie or misrepresent the truth. Unreliable narrators mislead the audience and skew the story.

Unreliable narrators show the importance point-of-view has in a story. This is how the audience views the narrative, characters, conflict and action. Every story has unique perspective, some even have multiple. Clarifying this view is critical to telling the story effectively.

Most stories are told from either first or third-person points of view. The primary difference is whether the narrator takes an active role within the story. The same story can take a completely different tone when shifting from first to third-person, or vice versa.

The books of the Bible were written in different points of view— some in first-person and some in third-person. Certain passages of Paul's letters are even written in the second-person. They're directed at a specific audience.

Within some third-person stories, the narrators are omniscient or all-knowing. This may well be true for the tiny, fictional world of the story. But there is only one omniscient author in the nonfiction universe—God.

---

1   Spoiler alert

Although the Bible isn't written from His point of view, God's omniscience is mentioned often. He is the All-Knowing and All-Powerful Author of Creation.

God knows and understands everything within His story, even the number of stars in the sky. Yet, God also sees the world from our first-person perspective. He knows our thoughts and experiences. This makes Him the ultimate narrator.

A point of view is the lens through which the audience will experience your story. Turning the perspective one way or the other impacts how characters and plot points are perceived.

Whichever viewpoint you choose helps to direct and clarify a story's focus.

## PRAYER

God, thank You for giving us each a unique perspective. Our personal point of view gives us a singular take on the world. We each have our own story to tell.
Help us to understand the perspective of others so we might better understand how they view the world.

In your omniscience, help us to broaden our perspective and open our minds to new ideas and opinions. Give us a clear vision and an open heart. Amen.

## ACTION

Grab a story you've already created or one from someone else. Identify the story's point of view. Now rewrite the story from a different perspective.

This can go from first-person to third-person. Or vice versa. Or switch between characters. How does this shift in point of view change how the story is written?

# NOTES

# DAY 13

# VOICE

**BIG IDEA**: A storyteller's voice is their own unique identity and ability to craft a story.

Out of the heavens He let you hear His voice to discipline you; and on earth He let you see His great fire, and you heard His words from the midst of the fire.
—**Deuteronomy 4:36**

The voice of the Lord is over the waters; the God of glory thunders, the Lord thunders over the mighty waters. The voice of the Lord is powerful; the voice of the Lord is majestic. —**Psalms 29:3-4**

Ray Kinsella is a simple corn farmer. He lives in Iowa with his wife and young daughter. And he loves baseball. One day while walking through his corn field, Ray hears a disembodied voice.

"If you build it, he will come."[1]

Kinsella doesn't understand what this means until he sees a vision of a baseball field in the middle of the corn. He realizes that he needs to build a baseball diamond. Despite some trepidation from his wife, Ray builds that baseball field.

He soon becomes a joke in the community. Who builds a baseball field in a corn field? Neighbors urge Ray to see reason and abandon the dream. But he doesn't listen to them. Then the family hits financial trouble.

---

1 Field of Dreams. Dir. Phil Alden Robinson. Universal Pictures, 1989.

Dedicating the field to baseball instead of corn means lost income. The situation seems hopeless. Then, the ghosts of legendary baseball stars begin stepping out of the cornfields. And they start playing baseball.

These players include Ray's late father, John Kinsella. Ray and his father never had a good relationship. He realizes that this is his opportunity to reconcile with his dad.

Ray introduces his dead father to his family and then plays one last game of backyard catch with his dad. It's a family reunion that all started with a mysterious voice.

*Field of Dreams* is a powerful reminder of what we can accomplish when we listen to those crazy voices in our heads.

The Bible tells the story of Samuel who was helping to take care of the prophet Eli. One night, Samuel hears the voice of God calling for him. Mistaking God's voice for Eli's, Samuel runs into the prophet's room asking what he needs. Confused, Eli sends the boy back to bed.

This happens twice more until Eli realizes that Samuel is being called by the voice of God. He instructs Samuel to tell God he is listening. Samuel does what he's told and receives instruction straight from God.

A storyteller's voice is their control over the language. For some storytellers, that's a well-defined pattern of words and tone.

Voice gives identity to the storyteller. It's your personal thumbprint on the story. And it can take a long time to discover. Years of practice and dedication have to occur before storytellers are able to unearth and refine their voice.

Voice plays a meaningful role in the impact of any given story. Even the best plot line can falter with a weak voice. Or, the mundane can be woven into a riveting story by the right storyteller. It's all about voice and how the story is told.

There's a difference between a style and voice. Styles are more general and can apply to many storytellers. A voice is uniquely your own. Voice is what helps you tell the difference between novels written by Dr. Seuss or Stephen King.

The Bible was written by many authors over a long period of time. So God's narrative combines many different voices together.

In most cases, this would lead to one confusing and inconsistent story. But each of these books was inspired by God who lends His voice to the biblical scribes.

This unified inspiration gives the Bible an undertone of consistency. While there may be a variety of voices speaking in the biblical narrative, they're all singing the same tune. These unique voices combine together into one greater story about God. He spoke to them that they may tell His tale.

Discovering the power of one's voice is a process. It's done through trial and error. Only by using our voices can we find them. Listening to the Word of God can strengthen our voice.

## PRAYER

God, thank You for giving each of us a voice. Help us to find that voice and use it to join in telling Your greater story. Our voice is what makes us unique from one another. Give us the determination to find our voice. Give us the strength to use it. Give us the wisdom to use them for Your purposes. Amen.

## ACTION

Pick a story you've written and read it out loud. Listen to how your voice sounds as you read it. This is one of the best ways to identify the tone of your voice in your writing. (It's also a good editing technique to find awkwardly worded sentences or grammatical errors.)

Now get a friend to read the same story aloud. Does this change how you perceive the story at all? What are some other ways that you can develop and perfect your own unique storytelling voice?

# NOTES

# DAY 14

# SETTING

**BIG IDEA**: Setting establishes a story's context of both time and place.

> The Lord, the God of heaven, who brought me out of my father's household and my native land and who spoke to me and promised me on oath, saying, 'To your offspring I will give this land'—He will send His angel before you so that you can get a wife for my son from there. —**Genesis 24:7**

> Jesus said to them, "Surely you will quote this proverb to me: 'Physician, heal yourself!' And you will tell me, 'Do here in your hometown what we have heard that you did in Capernaum.' "Truly I tell you," He continued, "no prophet is accepted in his hometown." —**Luke 4:23-24**

Author William Faulkner set most of his novels in Yoknapatawpha County, Mississippi. In the Chickasaw language, *yoknapatawpha* means "split land."

The central Mississippi county is home to more than 25,000 people. The county's largest and capitol city is Jefferson.

The only problem with Yoknapatawpha County—other than the difficulty in spelling it—is that it doesn't exist. Faulkner invented the fictional county for the sole purpose of his stories.

Yoknapatawpha is based primarily on Lafayette County, where Faulkner grew up. The city of Jefferson was inspired by Faulkner's hometown of Oxford.

Through his stories, Faulkner detailed the history, landscape and people of Yoknapatawpha. He drew fictional maps of the place. Scholars have documented the imaginary background of the made-up Mississippi county.

If you didn't know any better, you might imagine Yoknapatawpha County was a real place.[1]

Jesus' ministry took Him across Israel, performing miracles in city after city. As His legend grew, people flocked to Jesus to hear His teaching and be healed. Everywhere He went, people were in awe of Christ. That is, until His travels brought Jesus back to His hometown of Nazareth.

In Nazareth, the people weren't impressed. They had watched Jesus grow up. They were more familiar with Him as a willful youth than as the Messiah. They were skeptical about His miracles and teaching.

In fact, when Christ rebuked them for their doubt, the town of Nazareth tried to throw Him off a cliff!

Why did William Faulkner invent a county with a long name instead of writing about a real place? Why was Jesus worshiped in one city and doubted in the next?

Because Oxford and Nazareth were their hometowns. And our hometowns hold a different context for each of us.

Setting matters. Setting tells us the time and place of a story. It gives us the crucial details of context. Setting provides your audience a frame of mind to consider the story within.

A story written in a historical setting will have a much different tone than a story set in the future. A story set in the United States will have different expectations than one set in outer space.

Some of the place names and cultural references within the Bible are lost on a modern audience. Most of us aren't familiar with the cities mentioned in scripture or the historical culture of the time.

---

1 That level of realism goes to show the power of great storytelling.

But they had meaning to their author and original audience. For us, these settings reveal deeper truths when we learn more about their context.

Jesus was rejected at Nazareth because they were familiar with Him. They knew His mother and father. How could the son of a carpenter be the Son of God? Realizing the context of their dismissal of Christ gives it clarity.

The one consistency in the biblical settings and in each of our settings today is the presence of God. Because He is everywhere and exists forever. He resides in every setting.

It's amazing to think that the God who carried out the wonders told in the Bible still dwells with us today.

## PRAYER

God, thank You for the time and place into which each of us was born. The setting of our lives provides context as we search for meaning and purpose.

Without this setting, our the story of our lives would be vastly different. Remind us that You created all settings, and You exist everywhere. Regardless of where we've been and where we are going, we can always turn to You. Amen.

## ACTION

Take a classic story and change the setting. Adjust either the time, place or both. Imagine what it would be like if Robin Hood's adventures took place in outer space. Or if *To Kill A Mockingbird* happened in the age of the dinosaurs.

Besides being hilarious, how does this impact the story? How will the characters act differently in the new setting? Rewrite a scene from the story you've chosen within the context of your new setting. See how it plays out and why setting is so important.

# NOTES

# MOTIF

**BIG IDEA**: A motif summarizes a story's main themes and ideas.

> "Love the Lord your God with all your heart and with all your soul and with all your mind and with all your strength.' The second is this: 'Love your neighbor as yourself.' There is no commandment greater than these."
> **—Mark 12:30-31**

> "For God so loved the world that He gave His one and only Son, that whoever believes in Him shall not perish but have eternal life. For God did not send His Son into the world to condemn the world, but to save the world through Him." **—John 3:16-17**

> "A new command I give you: Love one another. As I have loved you, so you must love one another. By this everyone will know that you are my disciples, if you love one another." **—John 13:35-36**

The Bennett family has five unmarried daughters: Jane, Elizabeth, Mary, Kitty and Lydia. The family is running low on cash and could get cast out of their house upon their father's death. So Mrs. Bennett encourages the girls to all marry rich.

There are quite a few bachelors in the neighborhood: Mr. Bingley, Mr. Darcy, Mr. Collins and Mr. Wickham. While all of these fellows are attracted to the Bennett sisters, not all of them have enough money to satisfy their mother.

Amidst a series of parties, Mr. Darcy falls in love with Elizabeth. Unfortunately, his prejudice in believing that she is beneath his social class causes him to give Elizabeth an unsatisfactory marriage proposal.

Her pride prevents her from accepting his proposal, even though she loves him. Eventually, Mr. Darcy and Elizabeth move past their pride and prejudice and become happily engaged.

Jane Austen stuck two of the story's most important story motifs into the title of *Pride and Prejudice*. Pride and prejudice are the two overarching subjects that summarize the conflict in Austen's novel. Who would have guessed?

Motifs are a set of central concepts that define what the story is about and what makes it important. A motif gives a story consistency. It provides a single idea to build upon and deepen. Motifs provide a summary focal point for any story.

When the pharisees asked Jesus what the greatest commandment in the law was, they didn't expect an answer. Jesus' response blew them away. He instructed them to love God with all your heart, soul and mind. He also added that you should also love your neighbor as yourself.

Why is this important? Because these two commands summarize the entire Bible. One of the best ways to discover a story's theme is to condense it into a single sentence or word. Looking at Jesus' Great Commandment, one word seems to stand out as significant—love.

Love appears as the common, unifying theme throughout scripture. There are plenty of other recurring concepts in the Bible, but the one that stands out above all others is love.

Read the three verses above. These are three of the foundational verses in the gospels. Jesus explains that two of the greatest commandments both involve loving others.

God's love for us explains why He sent His only Son to die. Our love for one another reflects the love we have been shown. Love is the Bible's connecting thread. Love is the Bible's motif.

Much of the biblical story hinges on the sin and disobedience of

God's people. Time and time again, they turned away from Him. Despite this, God's love for us is unconditional.

Because of our sin, God sent Christ to die in our place. That act of love gives meaning to the rest of the biblical story. Past, present and future are defined by that love.

Some motifs are as simple as a single word. Some are more complex. The easier the motif is for your audience to understand the more powerfully it will stick with them. And the concept of God's love for us is one of the most powerful ideas of all.

## PRAYER

God, thank You that the overlying theme of Your story is one of love. You love us unconditionally, uncontrollably and inexplicably. Anyone who reads scripture and understands Your will can see that clearly.

You make Your love plain to us by repeating it again and again in Your story. Help us to remember that and to hold to the promise that You love us. Thank You for loving us and making Your love such an integral part of Your great narrative. Amen.

## ACTION

Select a story you've written or one of your favorites written by someone else. Now, summarize that story into a single sentence. What is the story really about? Take it one step further by boiling the entire story down to one or two words.

Don't get caught up in the specifics of characters and settings—focus on the universal truth at the core of the story. How does this motif drive the story? What makes this single motif so significant?

# NOTES

# BACKSTORY

**BIG IDEA**: A character's backstory explains the motivation for their actions.

> In those days Caesar Augustus issued a decree that a census should be taken of the entire Roman world. This was the first census that took place while Quirinius was governor of Syria. And everyone went to their own town to register.
>
> So Joseph also went up from the town of Nazareth in Galilee to Judea, to Bethlehem the town of David, because he belonged to the house and line of David. He went there to register with Mary, who was pledged to be married to him and was expecting a child.
>
> While they were there, the time came for the baby to be born, and she gave birth to her firstborn, a son. She wrapped Him in cloths and placed Him in a manger, because there was no guest room available for them.
> **—Luke 2:1-7**

Once upon a time, there lived a husband and wife named Jor-El and Lara on the planet Krypton. They were the proud parents of a baby boy named Kal-El.

Then, they learned that their planet was going to be destroyed. Kal-El's parents loaded their infant son into a spaceship and launched it in time to save his life.

The ship carrying the infant crash landed light years away on the planet Earth. The ship and baby inside were discovered by Jonathan and Martha Kent, who raised the boy as their own. They named him

Clark.

In case you weren't already aware, that's the origin story for the super-hero Superman. It's also influenced by the story of Moses. Both men were given up by their parents to save their lives. Both men would go on to be heroes in a foreign land.

Most superheroes have similar origin stories.

Bruce Wayne watched a thief murder his parents, which led him to fight criminals as Batman. Peter Parker transformed into Spider-Man after a radioactive spider bit him. Barry Allen was dosed with lightening-struck chemicals and became The Flash.

To have depth, characters in every story need some amount of background information. This is called a backstory.

It's the background information that tells the audience what led up to this point. It's what will be important to know during the narrative. It gets us up to speed and fills in the gaps.

Remember to only provide relevant information in a backstory. We don't need to know everything about the character. Don't overload so much information that the story gets muddled. Summarize the important stuff and get to the action.

Because the Bible is historical nonfiction, much of it is backstory. There are plenty of long lists of names and places that explain who went where and when. It builds toward something greater—the introduction of our protagonist, Jesus.

The trials and challenges of the Israelites magnify Jesus' life and crucifixion. The backstory of the Old Testament puts Jesus' ministry into perspective. It shows humanity's need for a Savior.

Even the story of Jesus' parents and their journey to Bethlehem gives Christ's birth meaning. It shows that the Messiah entered the world in the most humble way possible. He was born to a virgin, through the line of David, as foretold in the Old Testament.

You can use backstory in a similar way. Use the previous life experience of characters to show why the actions of the story are important. Give context to present action through the lens of past knowledge.

When done right, providing a character's backstory helps the audience see the bigger picture of your story.

## PRAYER

God, thank You for giving us the background of the story that led to the life of Your son. This information puts the significance of His sacrifice into context. Help us to see the Bible as a backstory to Jesus' life and a means to understanding His circumstances.

This background sheds light on our own situations. It shows how we can craft our future knowing the sacrifices that were made for us in the past. Amen.

## ACTION

Invent your own backstory for a made-up superhero. What are their super powers? Where did they get these powers? Do they have a sidekick? An arch-nemesis?

Answer these questions and any others that adoring fans might ask in the hero's backstory. You can do the same for nearly any character in a story. Even if these details don't make it into the final narrative, they still help flesh out the person in your mind.

# NOTES

# DAY 17

# FORESHADOWING

**BIG IDEA**: Foreshadowing builds anticipation for the story's coming action.

> "I will send my messenger, who will prepare the way before me. Then suddenly the Lord you are seeking will come to His temple; the messenger of the covenant, whom you desire, will come," says the Lord Almighty.
> —**Malachi 3:1**

> He then began to teach them that the Son of Man must suffer many things and be rejected by the elders, the chief priests and the teachers of the law, and that He must be killed and after three days rise again.
> —**Mark 8:3**

Italy is well known for its organized crime families and the conflicts between these rivals. Nowhere in literature is this more evident than the feud between the Montagues and the Capulets. We're never told why they're feuding, just that they hate each other's guts.

Enter Romeo, a young man from the Montague line. He's so infatuated with a girl named Rosaline that he's willing to crash a Capulet party in disguise to see her. Before he and his buddies get to the masquerade, Romeo engages in a monologue.

> My mind misgives some consequence yet hanging in the stars shall bitterly begin his fearful date with this night's revels and expire the term of a despised life closed in my breast.[1]

---

1   Act 1, Scene 4

In case you don't speak Shakespearean, this translates to: "I've got a bad feeling about this. And I might die soon." Even so, Romeo ignores the ominous foreshadowing and goes to the party anyway.

Instead of Rosaline, Romeo meets another girl named Juliet. The only problem is she's a member of the Capulet clan. Regardless, he decides to woo her below her balcony. While talking to Juliet, Romeo proclaims:

> Life were better ended by their hate, than death pro-
> rogued, wanting of thy love.[1]

Essentially, he would rather die than not be able to love Juliet.[2] Conveniently enough, he gets his wish. Romeo and Juliet are able to marry in secret, but both end up killing themselves, out of desperation, by the end of the play. It's almost as if Romeo predicted it.

Romeo and Juliet's deaths shouldn't come as a shock to you. Partially because William Shakespeare wrote the famous play back in 1597. But also because their deaths are foreshadowed many times during the play. It would have been more of a surprise if they hadn't died.

Foreshadowing is any hint of a future event within a story. It's as if these looming plot points are casting a dark shadow that reaches earlier parts of the story.

By using foreshadowing, storytellers can build up to a bigger moment while also drawing readers in. This creates a sense of anxious suspense until the moment of impact.

Foreshadowing manifests itself in the Bible in the form of prophets. God used prophets to guide his people. These prophets foretold many things, including the coming of plagues and hardships. God spoke to them about such things to warn the Israelites.

Among these prognostications, these godly messengers also prophesied about a Messiah. This Savior would come to fulfill God's covenant and save His people from death.

---

1   Act 2, Scene 2
2   Talk about dramatic teenagers.

The prophet Isaiah talked a lot about Immanuel, who would be born of a virgin, heal the sick and claim the throne of David. Wonder who that could have been referring to?

These Old Testament prophets were spread out over hundreds of years. But they were all hinting at the coming arrival of mankind's Savior. By the time Jesus was born, the Israelites were prepared for His big entrance.

Jesus Himself used foreshadowing in two significant instances—to predict His death and Peter's denial. Jesus hinted at these two things. Both predictions were doubted by the disciples. Both predictions came true.

To Jesus, these weren't predictions as much as facts. He knew that they would happen. God knew that His son would come to save the world. God knows how the story goes because He wrote it. He knew what these events foreshadowed, because He put the events into place.

As storytellers, we're privileged to know what's coming next in the story. We can give the audience hints to keep them interested and guessing. Using foreshadowing builds up anticipation and makes the big reveal even more satisfying.

## PRAYER

God, thank You for designating prophets to guide us toward You. Thank You for speaking through them to point the way toward Jesus. During His life, Jesus spoke of the power His sacrifice could have in our lives.

Give us the clarity to see how these truths can shape our future. And give us the wisdom to believe that You are faithful to provide the future You promised. Amen.

## ACTION

Re-read a story or re-watch a movie you already know has a climactic or twist ending. Be on the lookout for clues the storyteller left behind that point to the ending. It's easier to spot these when you're already aware what's going to happen. How can you use foreshadowing in your own storytelling to build up anticipation for the end?

## NOTES

# DAY 18

# PLOT TWIST

**BIG IDEA**: A plot twist relies on surprise to increase the impact of a story's climax.

> Very early on the first day of the week, just after sunrise, they were on their way to the tomb and they asked each other, "Who will roll the stone away from the entrance of the tomb?" But when they looked up, they saw that the stone, which was very large, had been rolled away. As they entered the tomb, they saw a young man dressed in a white robe sitting on the right side, and they were alarmed.
>
> "Don't be alarmed," He said. "You are looking for Jesus the Nazarene, who was crucified. He has risen! He is not here. See the place where they laid Him. But go, tell His disciples and Peter, 'He is going ahead of you into Galilee. There you will see Him, just as He told you.'" Trembling and bewildered, the women went out and fled from the tomb. They said nothing to anyone, because they were afraid. —**Mark 16:2-8**

The climax of Star Wars' *The Empire Strikes Back* finds Luke Skywalker facing off in a light saber duel against the dreaded Darth Vader.

In the previous film, Vader had murdered Skywalker's mentor, Obi Wan Kenobi, in a similar duel. Before his death, Kenobi had shared with Luke that Vader had betrayed and murdered Luke's father during the Clone Wars.

Needless to say, the young protagonist was unhappy with the film's helmeted villain. Luke carried a great deal of emotion and anguish into the fight. These emotions got slightly more complicated when Vader slices off Luke's hand and forces him to the edge of a precipice.

There, Vader tries to persuade Luke to join him on the Dark Side of the Force so that they can rule the galaxy together. Luke hurls back that he'll never become evil because Vader murdered his father.

It's then that Darth Vader delivers the famous line:

> "Luke, I *am* you father."[1]

Crazy, right? Only, that plot twist probably comes as no surprise to most of you. The gut-wrenching twist was a huge surprise when *The Empire Strikes Back* originally came out in 1980, but it's since become a well-known staple of pop culture.

In fact, one of the reasons I chose to use this as an example was because it is one of the few plot twists I could share with no fear of repercussions. There's no surprise left to spoil.

The same is true for the Bible's plot twists. We know exactly what's coming in most every major Bible story. Jesus' death is no surprise. But it certainly was to the contemporary audience. And our fore-knowledge of it shouldn't lessen its impact.

Over the years, the Israelites had a number of kings who led their nation. One of the primary roles of the king was leading the armies into battle. He was often a great warrior who led the Israelites to great victories over their numerous enemies.

As they turned away from God, the Israelites lost His favor and began losing battles to their enemies. Their kings became corrupt and their kingdom weakened.

The promise of a Messiah gave them hope that they would one day restore their former glory and retake the kingdom.

When that Savior was born, He was declared the King of Kings. Jesus

---

1    The Empire Strikes Back. Dir. George Lucas. Lucas Films, 1980.

was expected to take up the mantle held by His ancestor, King David, and resume the same kind of military conquest that came along with the title of king.

However, Jesus lived a much different life. He served people. He healed people. He hung out with the poor and even those who were despised, like prostitutes and tax collectors.

This certainly wasn't expected of the one they called the King of Kings. But even among His disciples, Jesus was expected to claim the throne of Israel and become a ruler here on Earth.

Imagine their shock and disappointment, when Jesus was captured and killed. For the Israelites, this was a twist of fate.

However, the real plot twist comes when Jesus rolled away the stone and rose from the grave. He defeated the enemies—sin and death—only He could. And not by fighting on a battlefield, but by sacrificing Himself in complete humility.

Plot twists surprise the audience in a way that they never see coming. The people of Israel expected an Earthly king, but the twist came when Jesus defeated death and ascended to Heaven as an eternal king.

This story was made all the more impactful because it was unexpected.

## PRAYER

God, thank You for giving us the king that we needed and not the king that we expected. We often think we know what we want, but praise You for giving us what we need.

It's only because of our lack of vision that we're surprised by the switch. Help us to better see Your plan for our lives and not lose faith when You send us an unexpected plot twist. Amen.

## ACTION

Plot twists don't happen by accident. They are planned in advance of creating a story. Think of all the great plot twists in stories. These are carefully crafted from the beginning to lead the audience into an unexpected resolution.

Can you write an entire story based off of a plot twist? Think of the twist first and then write backwards from there. See how difficult it is to keep the secret hidden from the audience until just the right moment.

## NOTES

# AUTHOR

**BIG IDEA**: An author has authority over a story, just as God has authority over creation.

> Many have undertaken to draw up an account of the things that have been fulfilled among us, just as they were handed down to us by those who from the first were eyewitnesses and servants of the word.
>
> With this in mind, since I myself have carefully investigated everything from the beginning, I too decided to write an orderly account for you, most excellent Theophilus, so that you may know the certainty of the things you have been taught. —**Luke 1:1-4**

Billy Pilgrim is a 21-year-old assistant chaplain in the US Army during World War II. He's a pacifist who hates the war and refuses to fight. He's tall and skinny and wants to be an optometrist when he leaves the war.

His battalion is captured by German forces during the Battle of the Bulge in 1944. They are taken to a prisoner of war camp in Dresden where they are housed in a converted cattle slaughterhouse and forced to do labor for the German army.

One night while walking by the latrines, Pilgrim overhears a fellow POW puking his brains out. This was Billy's only encounter with the man, but it still had a major impact on Billy's story.

Here's how the man is described:

"That was I. That was me. That was the author of this

book."[1]

That's right. Kurt Vonnegut wrote himself in his own book. This is appropriate considering that *Slaughterhouse-Five* is a semi-autobiographical novel. Even if it's also partially science fiction.

Vonnegut actually saw the firebombing of Dresden as a POW during WWII. Most of the characters in the novel are based on real people. The emotions involved with describing the war are real, even if the aliens who put Billy Pilgrim in an intergalactic zoo are fictional.

Vonnegut put himself into a few of his other books, but never in a major role. He always hovers on the periphery of the plot, observing and narrating. This self-insertion helps us to understand how an author can impact and have an active role in a story.

The Bible has quite a few authors—Noah, David, Solomon, Matthew, John, Luke and Paul, to name a few. It took about 40 authors to write the whole thing—about 30 in the Old Testament and 10 in the New Testament.

Moses recorded most of the first five books—Genesis, Exodus, Leviticus, Deuteronomy and Numbers. King David composed many of the Psalms. His son, Solomon, wrote Proverbs. Paul penned quite a few letters to churches around the world that are included as books in the New Testament.

Many of the books—like all four gospels—bear the individual author's name. Some of these authors were involved in the stories they wrote about, like Matthew and John. Others, like Luke, compiled their narrative through careful research and study.

As different characters have different points of view, authors have different storytelling voices. Each of the various biblical writers brought in his own experience and perspective.

So how were these 40 authors, spread out over the course of 1,500 years, able to come up with a comprehensive story? Because a single

---

1   Vonnegut, Kurt (12 January 1999). Slaughterhouse-Five. Dial Press Trade Paperback. p. 160.

author was working through them—God. His divine Spirit was the muse that inspired each of the authors to write.

It's no coincidence that the words *author* and *authority* come from the same root. An author has authority over the creation of a story in the same way that God wields creative power over the Earth.

In the stories we write, we are the creators. We have the power over the stories to change what we want and need. God holds the same power over the entire world. Our lives are His masterpiece.

By acting as storytellers, we're mimicking God's creative work.

## PRAYER

God, thank You for being the author of creation. Thank You for writing the greatest story ever told. Only You could have assembled the Bible, written by dozens of authors, scattered over hundreds of years. It was Your will that they write and that we read their story. May the stories we write reflect the glory of Your greater story. Amen.

## ACTION

Retell a story you experienced firsthand. You can tell it from your perspective or a completely different point of view. Feel free to take creative liberties to stretch the truth and create a new experience.

Consider how you impact every story you write. What experiences and perspectives affect how the story is told? As objective as we may try to be, authors always influence their work.

We can't help but leave our fingerprints on the stories we create—even God is the same way. What traces of yourself do you imprint on your stories?

# NOTES

# AUDIENCE

**BIG IDEA**: Know your audience because who you're speaking to impacts what you say.

> Many seek an audience with a ruler, but it is from the Lord that one gets justice. —**Proverbs 29:26**

> I write to you, dear children, because you know the Father. I write to you, fathers, because you know Him who is from the beginning. I write to you, young men, because you are strong, and the word of God lives in you, and you have overcome the evil one.
> —**1 John 2:12-14**

**M**eet Rosencrantz and Guildenstern. They are childhood friends of Hamlet, the prince of Denmark. They're an odd pair who get into arguments about mortality, fate and the nature of reality.

Think of them as a 17ᵗʰ century version of Abbott and Costello.

After the king of Denmark summons them, the pair visit their royal buddy Hamlet at the palace. There, Rosencrantz and Guildenstern debate whether they have free will.

> ROSENCRANTZ leaps up and bellows at the audience.
> ROSENCRANTZ: Fire!
> (GUILDENSTERN jumps up.)
> GUILDENSTERN: Where?
> ROSENCRANTZ: It's all right—I'm demonstrating the misuse of free speech. To prove that it exists. (He regards the audience, that is the direction, with contempt—and other directions, then front again.) Not a move. They

should burn to death in their shoes.[1]

Rosencrantz is somehow aware he's in a play called *Rosencrantz and Guildenstern Are Dead*. He knows that there's an audience watching said play. And he knows it's inappropriate to yell "Fire!" in a crowded theater.

Tom Stoppard based his play on two minor characters from Shakespeare's *Hamlet*. He used these characters to make a commentary on theatrical audiences.

A character in a play or film who speaks directly to the audience is breaking the fourth wall. This is because there are three walls on a stage—two on either side of the actors and one behind them. Separating the actors from the audience is an imaginary fourth wall.

Having an actor address the crowd of spectators shatters the illusion that the play is real. It reminds the audience that the play is a play and the actors are actors. Not only that, it shows that the actors know they are actors who know that they're in a play. Crazy, meta stuff.

All this goes to show that an audience impacts the story. What would a play be like without an audience to watch it? Stories that are aware of their audience can do a better job of storytelling.

Who you're speaking to can be as important as what you're saying.

Knowing our audience helps us to craft the story so that it resonates with that group. Age, gender, language and country all shape an audience's perception of a story. The more audiences relate to a story, the closer it meets their expectations and understanding.

Most of the biblical authors were aware of their primary audience. They knew that the contemporary crowd would understand the context of their stories. The audience got all the cultural references and inside jokes.

Because much of the New Testament was written in the form of

---

1   Act 2, Line 70

letters, the writers had a specific audience in mind. Paul's letters were directed at the churches in Rome, Corinth and Ephesus (among others). Each letter spoke to their specific issues and needs.

We are not the primary audience of the Bible. We live thousands of years later, in different countries, speaking different languages. Yet, somehow, much of the Bible still has meaning to us.

That's because we are God's audience. The books of the Bible was originally intended to be read by a different group. But God knew all along that it would reach a much wider audience.

This is important to keep in mind as we craft our stories as well. Although we may have a distinct audience in mind, it may impact a much larger group than we expected. Telling stories with universal truths can reach audiences of all shapes and sizes.

## PRAYER

God, thank You for making us the audience for Your story. We are both a part of this on-going narrative and the intended audience to watch it play out. You crafted this story in such a way that it resonates with anyone who cares to listen. Help us to open our hearts to the impact this story has to offer. Helps us to hear the story that You are writing for us. Amen.

## ACTION

Write a letter to your audience from a character in a story. What would this character say if he or she was aware that they were in the story? How would they talk to someone who was experiencing the story?

Think about how that audience impacts how the story is told. Change this audience for a second. How does switching up their demographics force you to change the story?

# NOTES

# CLIMAX

**BIG IDEA**: The more you build up to a story's climax, the greater the potential payoff.

> These things happened to them as examples and were written down as warnings for us, on whom the culmination of the ages has come. —**1 Corinthians 10:11**

> In Him, we have redemption through His blood, the forgiveness of sins, in accordance with the riches of God's grace that He lavished on us. With all wisdom and understanding, He made known to us the mystery of His will according to His good pleasure, which He purposed in Christ, to be put into effect when the times reach their fulfillment—to bring unity to all things in heaven and on earth under Christ. —**Ephesians 1:7-10**

In the rural Indiana town of Hickory, Norman Dale is named the local high school basketball coach. Fresh from the Navy, Dale is adamant about discipline and fundamentals. This doesn't sit well with his new basketball team, who is still fond of their previous coach.

The small town is fanatic about basketball. There is a great deal of pressure on Dale to succeed in his new role. The citizens even hold a town hall meeting to decide whether he should be allowed to coach.

Through hard work, Dale is able to earn the trust and respect of his team and the town. They're able to build on the fundamentals to win games and advance to the regional tournament. That's where Coach Dale delivers a rousing locker room speech.

Don't get caught up thinking about winning or losing

this game. If you put your effort and concentration into playing to your potential, to be the best that you can be, I don't care what the scoreboard says at the end of the game, in my book we're gonna be winners.[1]

Thus inspired, Hickory advances to the state finals against the defending champions. The other team is taller, faster and more experienced. Hickory wins the championship on a last second shot, shocking the state and themselves.

If you haven't already recognized it, this is the plot to the movie *Hoosiers*. The film may have become clichéd, but clichés work. The story builds up to the climax of the championship game—delivering a victory for the underdogs.

It might seem an odd comparison, but the Bible's climax actually has some things in common with *Hoosiers*.

They're both about a small band of misfits from the middle of nowhere. They're both led by an unpopular guy who's almost run off by the authorities. But they both result in victory for the home team.

The first half of the Bible is a gradual build up for Jesus' arrival. Throughout the Old Testament, the Israelites are waiting for the promised Savior. God's chosen people continued to wander far from Him, in search for a leader who would bring them triumph.

As it turned out, Christ is the redeemer that the Israelites were waiting for. He was the answer to the promises that God had made for generations. That's why the gospel stories of Jesus' life and ministry serve as the biblical climax. It's what the story is all about.

This teaches us a valuable lesson of storytelling—the more you build up to a climax, the more potential it has to be rewarding. This build up isn't always measured in number of years or pages in a book. It's all about how much expectation you can drive home in your audience.

Not every story delivers on the hype. A disappointing climax under-

---

1   Hoosiers. Dir. David Anspaugh. Orion Pictures, 1986.

cuts all the work that went into the build up. But Jesus is the perfect climax to the biblical story.

His life, death and resurrection was the ultimate fulfillment of the promises God made to His chosen people.

The most satisfying stories showcase the story's conflict. They show how the characters developed through the narrative. An effective climax pulls together the important elements of the story into one big crescendo.

The Bible is unique because it has a climax that never truly ends. Christ rose from the grave and still reigns today. Because of that, we have an opportunity to play a part in the climax. God's story involves the culmination of all His people.

## PRAYER

God, thank You for giving us a resolution to Your story of creation that never ends. Thank You for bringing Christ into the world at the peak of Your story and allowing Him to be the focus of our narrative.

Jesus is the climax that was well worth the anticipation and waiting. He is the peak of a story that never ends. Because of that, we have the chance to be a part of the story's climax. Amen.

## ACTION

Think of your favorite climactic scene from a movie or chapter from a book. Give a brief description of what happened in the climax to make it so remarkable. What is the one moment that really sticks with you?

Then, trace a line back to at least three plot elements that built up to the climax. How did the tension built in the narrative come bubbling up at the peak moment?

# NOTES

# DAY 22

# EMOTION

**BIG IDEA**: The best stories are those that elicit great emotion.

> "Where have you laid him?" He asked.
> "Come and see, Lord," they replied.
> Jesus wept. Then the Jews said, "See how He loved him!"
> **—John 11:34-36**

Is there any more heartbreaking scene in animation than when Bambi's mother dies? It doesn't matter how old you are or how many times you've seen the film. It's hard not to tear up when the cartoon deer is shot and killed by a faceless hunter.

However, the story behind the story is perhaps even more tragic.

In 1938, Walt Disney was enjoying the financial success of several motion pictures. Disney decided to use some of his new-found wealth to buy a new home for his parents in California. They loved the new home, but unbeknownst to anyone, the house's furnace leaked fumes.

One night, Disney's mother, Flora, died in her sleep because of the toxic fumes. Although it wasn't his fault, Disney blamed himself for his mother's death. The accident haunted him for the rest of his life.

These emotions manifested themselves in stories like *Bambi*. In fact, the death of a character's parents is a recurring theme in many Disney stories.

Some characters have a father, but no mother—Ariel, Belle, Jasmine, Pocahontas, Nemo. Even more characters are orphans—Aladdin, Peter Pan, Tarzan, Mowgli, Anna and Elsa.

Although these deaths bring sadness to each tale, they also introduce other emotions, too. Long time Disney producer, Don Hahn, explained why these circumstances heighten the emotions of each story.

> Disney films are about growing up. They're about that day in your life when you have to accept responsibility. In shorthand, it's much quicker to have characters grow up when you bump off their parents... It's a story shorthand.[1]

The loss of loved ones also plays an emotional role in many biblical stories. Lazarus of Bethany was a friend and follower of Jesus. While traveling, Christ gets word that Lazarus has grown deathly ill.

By the time Jesus arrives to see His friend, Lazarus has already passed away. Christ was overcome with emotion.

His weeping is the shortest verse in the Bible. Those two words convey so much because they humanize Jesus. They show that God's Word made flesh had the same feelings all people do.

It's no coincidence that the overarching motif of the Bible—love—is an emotion. Great stories make you feel something—fear, hatred, empathy, even hunger. What makes them great is their ability to stir something deep inside us. Stories have the power to connect on an emotional level.

The best stories are able to make us feel several emotions, even all at once. It's what transforms a story from a simple narrative into a full experience. It's what makes us cry at romances, laugh at comedies and tremble in fear at horror.

The Bible itself commands a range of emotions. We are called to fear God, but also to love Him. There are plenty of biblical figures that we hate, and others we pity. The Bible's tone is serious, but there are the occasional light-hearted and funny moments.

---

1  Radloff, Jessica. "Why Don't Disney Heroines Have Mothers? The Real Reason Will Shock You." Glamour. Glamour Magazine, 10 Sept. 2014.

Most importantly, the Word of God is meant to bring us two senses—joy and hope. Joy at the life God has given us and hope for a better tomorrow. These are two powerful emotions that the biblical story evokes in each of its readers.

Emotion is the lasting connection that gives stories their power. Emotions help stories to transform our minds. Stories that are able to make us feel something tend to stick with us for the long haul.

## PRAYER

God, thank You for giving us a story that evokes an emotional response. Thank You for making it part of our fabric to connect with and react to such stories.

Even Your Son, Jesus, felt human emotion. This is how we know that He understands our burdens. Help us to learn the value of these emotions and to use them for Your glory. Amen.

## ACTION

Pick one emotion that you're trying to evoke in your audience. How do you want them to feel after reading the story? The best stories can trigger a range of emotions, but sometimes it's easier to start with one.

Craft your story in a way that focuses on delivering this emotional response. Usually, the deeper you're able to dive into this one emotion, the complexity of other emotions will follow.

# NOTES

# SUSPENSION OF DISBELIEF

**BIG IDEA:** Suspension of disbelief allows the audience to put aside their doubts while experiencing a story.

> Now Thomas (also known as Didymus), one of the Twelve, was not with the disciples when Jesus came. So the other disciples told him, "We have seen the Lord!" But he said to them, "Unless I see the nail marks in His hands and put my finger where the nails were, and put my hand into His side, I will not believe."
>
> A week later His disciples were in the house again, and Thomas was with them. Though the doors were locked, Jesus came and stood among them and said, "Peace be with you!" Then He said to Thomas, "Put your finger here; see my hands. Reach out your hand and put it into my side. Stop doubting and believe."
>
> Thomas said to him, "My Lord and my God!" Then Jesus told him, "Because you have seen me, you have believed; blessed are those who have not seen and yet have believed." —**John 20:24-31**

At the climax of *Indiana Jones and the Last Crusade*, our brave hero has survived some ancient booby traps. He has emerged to face the final challenge between him and the Holy Grail. Except the challenge is a giant chasm—too far to jump.

Thankfully, Indiana Jones knews from his father's research (and a helpful bit of foreshadowing earlier in the film) that overcoming the last obstacle required a leap of faith. He understood that he had to believe his way over the abyss.

Closing his eyes for dramatic effect, Jones took a bold step into nothingness... only to have his foot land on solid rock. His faith allowed him to pass the test.

This story sounds like the biblical story when Jesus walks on water. To prove his own faith, Peter steps out of the boat and begins striding toward the Messiah.

It's only when Peter realized what he was doing that he started to sink. Ever the Savior, Jesus grabs Peter and asks him why he doubted. Peter needed to be more like Indiana Jones.

After Jesus rose from the grave, He began appearing to His disciples. Many of them were overcome with joy at the sight of Him. They began to spread the news that Jesus had returned.

One disciple distrusted their story. Thomas wanted to see Christ for himself before he would believe that Jesus was back. Thomas' doubt was understandable, but would earn him the nickname Doubting Thomas[1].

Sure enough, Jesus confronted Thomas and proved the story of His resurrection to be true. Christ allowed Thomas to place his finger into the holes in His hands. Jesus then called for Thomas to stop doubting and believe.

Stories often have unbelievable events in them. They require us to set aside our questions and go with what the author says. As the audience, we need to be willing to believe in the parameters of the story. Otherwise, we're never going to appreciate the narrative's message.

Our call to set aside our doubts when hearing a story is called the *Suspension of Disbelief.* Essentially, this asks us not to nitpick on the unessential details for the sake of enjoying the story as a whole. Let a

---

1    Probably better than the nicknames they were giving to Judas.

few minor plot holes slide and look at the bigger picture.

Thomas was so caught up in his disbelief that he missed the joy of Christ's return. When we fail to suspend our disbelief within the context of story, we may miss the message, too.

## PRAYER

God, doubt is a part of life. But help us to keep from being lost in doubt. Give us the strength to see through doubt and focus on Your promises. Thank You for forgiving us when we fail to believe and for forgiving our doubt. Thank You for not giving us any true cause to distrust Your authority and truth.

You've proven who You are and have been patient to any resistance we show in understanding that truth. Help us to not be distracted by our disbelief or risk missing the opportunity for faith. Amen.

## ACTION

Start with a nonfiction story—either from your own life or someone else's. Now add an element of fantasy into it. This could be a unicorn, magical abilities or finding buried treasure.

How might this fictional addition cause your audience to doubt? Try crafting the story in as believable a way as possible. As long as your new work of fiction is consistent, the burden of suspension of disbelief lies on the audience.

# NOTES

# DAY 24

# EPISTOLARY

**BIG IDEA**: Epistolaries are more personal stories written in the form of letters.

> You yourselves are our letter, written on our hearts, known and read by everyone. You show that you are a letter from Christ, the result of our ministry, written not with ink but with the Spirit of the living God, not on tablets of stone but on tablets of human hearts.
>
> Such confidence we have through Christ before God. Not that we are competent in ourselves to claim anything for ourselves, but our competence comes from God. He has made us competent as ministers of a new covenant—not of the letter but of the Spirit; for the letter kills, but the Spirit gives life. —**2 Corinthians 3:2-6**

In *The Screwtape Letters*, a senior demon by the name of Screwtape mentors a rookie devil, Wormwood. Their goal is to secure the damnation of an unnamed British gentleman, known only as The Patient.

Screwtape guides Wormwood in the ways of undermining faith and encouraging sinful behavior. Wormwood also seeks advice from his evil coach on navigating the complex bureaucracy of Hell.

Despite their best efforts, The Patient devotes his life to Christ. Wormwood and Screwtape's plans have been foiled.

C.S. Lewis tells his classic tale of temptation and sin in the form of letters (as the title would suggest). Each chapter is a correspondence from either Screwtape or Wormwood. It's not mentioned how these letters were delivered.[1]

These letters not only tell us the action of the story, but also they reveal the voice and character of both Screwtape and Wormwood. They provide a personal window into their minds.

This form of storytelling using letters is called *epistolary writing*. Through letters, storytellers can take on the perspective of a character, while speaking to a specific audience. This technique allowed Lewis to assume the voice of the enemy trying to ensnare a normal man.

Epistolaries are some of the oldest examples of literature. They can include letters, journal entries, newspaper articles, collected documents or emails. Classic examples of epistolary literature includes Bram Stoker's *Dracula*, and *The Diary of Anne Frank*.

Most of the New Testament is written in the form of letters. In fact, these books are sometimes referred to as The Epistles for that reason.

Many of the book titles reference the recipients of the Apostle Paul's letters. Romans was written to the church in Rome, Corinthians to the church in Corinth, and so on.

Because these correspondences were written to specific audiences, they each have a specific context. The letters contain detailed instructions personalized to these churches directly from Paul. He knew each of his audiences and wrote words with the intention of guiding and encouraging them.

The epistles differ from the more historical books of the Bible. They are more personal. They're written to a specific audience with specific words of encouragement. But their impact still carries weight with any who reads the words.

Although we are not the intended audience of these letters, we can still gain much insight through Paul's words. The letters are crafted in a way that communicates to a wider audience about a broader subject.

---

1    Presumably using the Hell Postal Service.

Screwtape and Wormwood's letters were not written to us. But they still tell us a great deal about the characters and ourselves.

The epistolary form of storytelling may not be as common as it once was, but it's still a powerful means of communicating a narrative. Letters can tell stories in a more personal way. Because letters themselves are personal.

## PRAYER

God, thank You for letters of encouragement and wisdom. Paul wrote many letters centuries ago that were not originally intended for us. Yet, those letters have survived the test of time and we can read and learn their insight still to this day.

Thank You for preserving those letters and guiding their words in the first place. Help us to encourage others with our words and use our correspondences to impact others. Amen.

## ACTION

Write a letter to one of your story's characters. It can be from you as the author of your story or as another one of the characters. What would you say to this character in the letter? How does the specific format of letter writing change how you tell a story?

# NOTES

# DAY 25

# UNIVERSAL TRUTHS

**BIG IDEA**: Universal truths make a story relevant well beyond its original time and place.

The fear of the Lord is the beginning of knowledge, but fools despise wisdom and instruction. —**Proverbs 1:7**

Show me Your ways, Lord, teach me Your paths. Guide me in Your truth and teach me, for You are God my Savior, and my hope is in You all day long. —**Psalm 25:4-5**

To the Jews who had believed him, Jesus said, "If you hold to my teaching, you are really my disciples. Then you will know the truth, and the truth will set you free." —**John 8:31-32**

Remember the end of *The Wizard of Oz*? The bumbling "wizard" floated away in a hot air balloon, leaving Dorothy stuck without a way home to Kansas.

Enter Glenda the Good Witch. She reveals that Dorothy had the ability to return home the whole time.[1] All Dorothy had to do was click her heels together three times and say the magic words:

"There's no place like home."[2]

She repeats the phrase in case the audience didn't catch that line as the theme of the film. It took running away from home for Dorothy to realize that home is better than a fantastical land filled with talking trees and flying monkeys.

---

1 Where was that information two hours ago?
2 The Wizard of Oz. Dir. Victor Fleming. Metro-Goldwyn-Mayer, 1933.

104

That's the moral of the story.

Aesop's fables are known for having a short, quotable moral at the end of each story. These morals summarize the universal truth at the heart of each fable. They explain to the audience why the story was important. There is no missing the lesson.

Not every story ends with an explicit moral. But the best stories have these same universal truths at their core. God could have written a witty and pithy moral at the end of each Bible story.

Instead, He wrapped up these truths within the story for us to find and uncover.

Universal truths are what make any story relevant beyond the time and place it was first told. Some stories hold a particular truth only meaningful to the original audience. But the stories built on a foundation of timeless principles lasts forever.

The Ten Commandments God gave to Moses on Mount Sinai weren't only written for the Israelites. God bestowed these commandments as a guide to live by for future generations. The Book of Proverbs contains amazing pieces of wisdom that are always applicable.

Jesus gave two commandments to His disciples—love God with everything you've got and love your neighbor as yourself.

These are two easy to remember and understand instructions that summarize all of the law and the prophets.

But these commandments were not meant only for those listening to Jesus that day. They are truths that apply to everyone, for all time.

Universal truths provide a connection to stories for all people at all times. The greater the truth, the more people will use the story for inspiration and understanding.

Give your story a deeper, lasting meaning with a universal truth.

## PRAYER

God, thank You for the clarity of biblical truths. Thank You for including countless universal messages within Your scriptures. We can relate to these truths even hundreds of years after they took place.

These truths are what make the Bible so timeless and valuable. Help us to see these truths when we read Your stories. And help us to understand how to apply them within the context of our lives. Amen.

## ACTION

Pick out a common saying or maxim. For example, "The early bird gets the worm," or "An apple a day keeps the doctor away." Now create a story based on this moral.

What deeper truths can you uncover through this simple truth? How can this truth give your story a longer shelf life? What can people learn from the story?

# NOTES

# DAY 26

# IMAGERY

**BIG IDEA**: Storytellers use imagery to paint a mental picture in the mind of the audience.

> I turned around to see the voice that was speaking to me. And when I turned I saw seven golden lampstands, and among the lampstands was someone like a son of man, dressed in a robe reaching down to His feet and with a golden sash around His chest. The hair on His head was white like wool, as white as snow, and His eyes were like blazing fire.
>
> His feet were like bronze glowing in a furnace, and His voice was like the sound of rushing waters. In His right hand, He held seven stars, and coming out of His mouth was a sharp, double-edged sword. His face was like the sun shining in all its brilliance. —**Revelation 1:12-16**

A passage from Ralph Ellison's *Invisible Man* describes the narrator buying a yam from a street vendor. The nameless main character moved to Harlem from the south, where yams are a common food.

For this reason, the yams remind the narrator of home. In New York, he's cold and tired and hungry and lost. The steaming hot, sticky sweet yams sold at the food cart are an escape from his harsh reality.

Ellison's description of the character eating the sweet potato is vivid enough to make any audience hungry.

> I took a bite, finding it as sweet and hot as any I'd ever had, and was overcome with such a surge of homesickness that I turned away to keep my control. I walked

along, munching the yam, just as suddenly overcome by an intense feeling of freedom — simply because I was eating while walking along the street. It was exhilarating.[1]

This is one of many illustrative passages in Ellison's master work. Sensory perception is so important because the main character feels so overlooked. He refers to himself as the invisible man because no one seems to see him.

Imagery is all about using words to create an image. The more detailed and precise the words, the clearer the image will be in the heads of your audience. It's no coincidence that *image* and *imagine* come from the same root word.

To imagine means to form a mental picture of something. Imagination is a person's capacity to form these images.

In the same way, the best stories are ones we can picture playing out in our minds. Storytelling involves transmitting a mental image into the minds of others through words.

The Book of Revelation is a vision revealed to the disciple John about the return of Jesus and the end of the Earth. Fun fact: the Greek word for revelation is *apokalypsis*. This is where we derive the term *Apocalypse* from.

As the last book of the Bible, Revelation is full of bizarre and mysterious symbolism. But it also contains some powerful imagery.

One of the highlights early in the text is John's encounter with the resurrected Christ. Different from Jesus as He walked the Earth, this is the Messiah in His full glory. It's difficult for John to look directly at Jesus, let alone describe how He looks in words.

The comparisons John uses to describe Christ's appearance seem impossible, yet poetic. His eyes are blazing fire, feet like glowing bronze, with a voice like rushing waters. These words match with the idea that Jesus is the Light of the World.

---

1   Ellison, Ralph. Invisible Man. N.p.: Random House, 1952. 264. Print.

It's hard to imagine what Jesus may have looked like to John in that moment. It's odd to think what a sharp, double-edged sword coming out of Jesus' mouth would look like. However, we still get a sense of the awe-inspiring majesty through John's words.

Detailed and descriptive imagery is used throughout the Bible. In almost every story, the authors are able to use a variety of language to paint a picture in our heads.

Using vivid and detailed language, storytellers can create an image in the audience's mind. The clearer the picture, the more likely it will be remembered.

## PRAYER

God, thank You for the vivid descriptions within scripture. These stories help us to picture these scenes and place ourselves in the narrative.

Thank You for the beautiful imagery that You inspired in the biblical authors. These stirring passages give us a connection to the stories and help us better understand what the story means. Amen.

## ACTION

Find a picture; it could be a favorite family photo or an ad clipped from a magazine. Now write a short story based on this image.

Focus on trying to transmit this photo into the mind of your audience. It may help to close your eyes and visualize the image. What do you see? How can you describe this mental image using words?

# NOTES

# DAY 27

# SYMBOLISM

**BIG IDEA**: Symbolism transforms ordinary objects into the embodiment of complex concepts.

> "When the woman saw that the fruit of the tree was good for food and pleasing to the eye, and also desirable for gaining wisdom, she took some and ate it. She also gave some to her husband, who was with her, and he ate it." —**Genesis 3:6**

> "Then I saw a Lamb, looking as if it had been slain, standing at the center of the throne, encircled by the four living creatures and the elders. The Lamb had seven horns and seven eyes, which are the seven spirits of God sent out into all the earth."
> —**Revelation 5:6**

The Pevensie children were seemingly normal in every way. Peter, Susan, Edmund and Lucy were sent to live with a regular, elderly professor in the boring British countryside.

During a routine game of hide-and-seek, the children discovered a magical kingdom inside of an otherwise ordinary wardrobe. Amazed, they immediately began exploring the wonders of Narnia.

During the exploration, Edmund encountered an evil witch. Fooled by her charms, Edmund promised to introduce her to his siblings. Secretly, the witch intended to kill the four children.

Talking beavers warned the other three Pevensie siblings about the witch. They learned that she had taken Edmund captive. The beavers entreated the children to seek help from the powerful lion, Aslan.

To save their brother's life, Aslan traded his life for Edmund's. The witch and her minions killed Aslan as the children watched, heartbroken. Yet, the magic that binds Narnia resurrected Aslan. The rules of their universe would not allow an innocent person (or lion) to die in the place of the guilty.

The reborn Aslan led the good guys in defeating the witch and restoring peace and happiness in Narnia.

*The Lion, the Witch and the Wardrobe* is a book intended for children. Yet, most children miss out on the hidden symbolism. They assume that returning from the dead is what magic talking lions do.

When reading *The Chronicles of Narnia* as an adult, the metaphors are all too clear. Aslan represents Christ, who gave Himself up for us, and conquered death to redeem us of our sins. Leave it to C.S. Lewis to sneak that subtle message into a series of books for kids.

In the garden of Eden, Adam and Eve ate an apple from the Tree of the Knowledge of Good and Evil. Since then, apples have come to represent much more than a piece of fruit. They symbolize the act of disobedience that brought original sin into the world.

Jesus is often referred to as the Lamb of God. His death on the cross mirrors the animal sacrifices made by the Israelites in the Old Testament. Like a sheep, Jesus remained silent and docile as He was led to the slaughter.

There are a great deal more symbols used throughout the Bible. The water of baptism represents washing away sin. The dove Noah sent from the ark and the olive branch it carried both mean peace. The Ichthys[1] represents Christianity because the first disciples were fishers of men.

Religions use symbolism frequently, but it's also an important storytelling technique. Symbolism uses common items to allude to larger, more complex concepts. This allows the story to work on many levels and take on depth.

---

1   That fish symbol Christians put on their car bumpers

This is one of the ways that we know God's presence within the biblical story. These symbols and metaphors don't happen by coincidence.

It isn't a coincidence that shepherds, who raised sheep for sacrifice, would be the ones who followed a star to the manger in Bethlehem. It's also not a coincidence that Christ would be called the Lamb of God and be a sacrifice Himself.

These elements show that there is something larger at work. It's the evidence of a Master Storyteller. By knowing what happens at the end of the story, God crafts a narrative strengthened by the power of symbolism.

## PRAYER

God, thank you for filling your story with symbols that give the story added meaning and depth. Help us to understand what each of these symbols mean and why they're important.

It's no coincidence that you placed them within your narrative. They give us hints and clues to what the ultimate resolution might be. When seen in the right way, these symbols help to point back to you and show your handiwork. Amen.

## ACTION

Pick a symbolic object and tell a story about it. The symbol can represent anything, as long as your audience understands what it means. Use it to allude to something deeper and more meaningful.

Not every story needs overt symbolism, but it can help convey a loaded message. How can this symbol connect your story to a universal truth?

# NOTES

# THE HERO'S JOURNEY

**BIG IDEA**: Many stories of heroes and adventure follow the same basic template called The Hero's Journey.

> David said to the Philistine, "You come against me with sword and spear and javelin, but I come against you in the name of the Lord Almighty, the God of the armies of Israel, whom you have defied. This day the Lord will deliver you into my hands, and I'll strike you down and cut off your head.
>
> This very day I will give the carcasses of the Philistine army to the birds and the wild animals, and the whole world will know that there is a God in Israel. All those gathered here will know that it is not by sword or spear that the Lord saves; for the battle is the Lord's, and He will give all of you into our hands."
>
> As the Philistine moved closer to attack him, David ran quickly toward the battle line to meet him. Reaching into his bag and taking out a stone, he slung it and struck the Philistine on the forehead. The stone sank into his forehead, and he fell face down on the ground. David triumphed over the Philistine with a sling and a stone; without a sword in his hand he struck down the Philistine and killed him.—**1 Samuel 17:45-50**

Harry Potter was an ordinary British orphan who lived in a cupboard under the stairs of his aunt and uncle's house. His life was utterly dull, until he received a letter of acceptance to Hogwarts School of Witchcraft and Wizardry.

The revelation that he was a wizard thrust Harry reluctantly from the normal world into a world of magic. A giant named Hagrid served as Harry's guide to this new world. Hagrid also told Harry about the evil wizard, Voldemort, who murdered Harry's parents.

At Hogwarts, Harry became friends with fellow rookie wizards, Ron and Hermione. He also became enemies with Draco Malfoy and a rogue troll. With the help of his new friends, Harry overcame the challenges posed by his new enemies.

At the end of their first year at Hogwarts, Harry and friends faced the ultimate test. They entered a dangerous area and grappled against even more challenges. Finally, Harry used his wizard training to fight the evil Voldemort.

You're likely already familiar with the beloved *Harry Potter* saga by now. The story of the boy wizard has common elements that echo in other stories in a variety of forms. These similarities are not a coincidence.

The J.K. Rowling's famous novels roughly follow a storytelling template called *The Hero's Journey*. The Hero's Journey is a trope that follows a familiar narrative pattern. It's found in myths, legends, novels, movies and even within the Bible.

Mythologist Joseph Campbell first formed the concept of The Hero's Journey[1] back in 1949. He noticed a distinct pattern within different legendary stories. Campbell explains that most heroic stories follow the same basic outline.

The Hero's Journey template begins with an ordinary hero. The hero reluctantly accepts a call to adventure. Before venturing out, the hero receives support from a mentor.

Then, the hero crosses a threshold of no return into the unknown. In the unknown, the hero encounters many challenges, ultimately leading to victory. The hero returns to the known world changed forever.

1   Campbell, Joseph (1949). The Hero with a Thousand Faces. Princeton: Princeton University Press.

Why is this storytelling framework so common?

Perhaps it's because this is a story told by God that leaks into other cultures. Throughout scripture, God uses many ordinary men and women to do incredible things. He provides them with mentors to push them across a threshold into the unknown. They face challenges, but are able to succeed with God's help.

The story of David and Goliath follows a similar pattern. So does the story of Moses leading his people out of Egypt. Biblical heroes from Samson to Joshua all share some part of The Hero's Journey.

God continues to use elements in The Hero's Journey in our own lives today. When we face adversity, we are called to trust God, knowing triumph and growth will be our reward. In the meantime, we can look back at these classic tales as a blueprint for how The Hero's Journey plays out.

## PRAYER

God, thank You for giving us heroes within the Bible to inspire us to do great things. The Hero's Journey is common within storytelling because Your work inspires us to be spiritual heroes.

We can learn from stories of other heroes. With Your guidance, we can overcome the adversity worthy of any story. Help us to follow in the footsteps of the heroes before us that we may glorify You. Amen.

## ACTION

Choose a story from your own life that matches The Hero's Journey framework. When was a time that your routine was changed by a call to adventure?

Who was your mentor that helped you along the way? What were the challenges? How were you changed as a result of these challenges? Elements of The Hero's Journey are found not only in fiction, but also in the real world.

# NOTES

# POETIC JUSTICE

**BIG IDEA**: When justice becomes poetic, it means characters get what they deserve.

> Haman went out that day happy and in high spirits. But when he saw Mordecai at the king's gate and observed that he neither rose nor showed fear in his presence, he was filled with rage against Mordecai. Nevertheless, Haman restrained himself and went home.
>
> Calling together his friends and Zeresh, his wife, Haman boasted to them about his vast wealth, his many sons, and all the ways the king had honored him and how he had elevated him above the other nobles and officials. "And that's not all," Haman added.
>
> "I'm the only person Queen Esther invited to accompany the king to the banquet she gave. And she has invited me along with the king tomorrow. But all this gives me no satisfaction as long as I see that Jew Mordecai sitting at the king's gate."
>
> His wife Zeresh and all his friends said to him, "Have a pole set up, reaching to a height of fifty cubits, and ask the king in the morning to have Mordecai impaled on it. Then go with the king to the banquet and enjoy yourself." This suggestion delighted Haman, and he had the pole set up. —**Esther 5:9-14**

Xerxes was king of the Persian Empire, which ruled over Israel for quite some time. King Xerxes had many wives, but he was in search of a beautiful woman for his queen.

After searching through the kingdom, Xerxes selected Esther, who was renown for her beauty, to be his queen. The king didn't know it, but Esther was Jewish. She was also an orphan and had been raised by her elderly cousin, Mordecai.

One day, Mordecai had a run in with one of the king's noblemen named Haman. Mordecai refused to kneel before Haman, which enraged Haman.

So angry in fact, that Haman began to plot his revenge against Mordecai and all Jewish people. He told the king that the Jews were a bunch of troublemakers. Haman insisted that the Jewish people be robbed of their property and exterminated from the Persian empire.

To top it all off, Haman erects a giant pole where he hopes to impale Mordeci.

At first, the king agrees and allows Haman to carry out his vengeful edict against the Jews. Horrified, Mordecai tells Esther of Haman's plan.

Esther goes to the king and reveals her Jewish heritage, her relation to Mordecai, and explains how Haman had been trying to undermine the king's authority. She knows admitting that she is Jewish is a risk, but Esther has the courage to stand up and protect her people.

Charmed by his queen, and unhappy with Haman's actions, King Xerxes orders to have Haman killed. The king's guards conveniently discover the handy pole already prepared for impaling.

And so Haman is executed by the very means he intended to kill Mordeci—impaled on a pole of his own creation.

This reversal of fortunes is often referred to as *poetic justice*. It's the idea that people get what they deserve—sometimes in an ironically fitting manner.

Poetic justice is satisfying because it shows some level of fairness in the world.

Haman is manipulative and jealously tries to kill an innocent man and eradicate an entire nation. Instead, his actions seal his own fate. This would be too great a coincidence to not have been planned by God as part of the story. It shows that our actions have consequences.

Poetic justice shows up in a few other ways within the Bible. But the story of Esther and Haman is one of the most fitting demonstrations of how God is just. The fact that the justice is a bit poetic only makes for a better story.

## PRAYER

God, thank You for the righteousness You bestow upon us. Help us to act justly in accordance with Your character. Thank You for showing us right from wrong. Help us understand between the two and always choose what is right.

Most importantly, thank You for Your mercy. Help us to give mercy to those around us. You paid the price for our sin so we did not have to bear to consequences of our inequity. Amen.

## ACTION

Pick a character you dislike from a story. Compose a scene that shows them getting some poetic justice. Find something which goes around that could come around.

Poetic justice is usually reserved for punishment. But it could also be reversed to reward a good character. Are there hints early within the story that could come back later to provide dramatic effect?

# NOTES

# DAY 30

# RESOLUTION

**BIG IDEA**: A story ends when the primary conflict comes to a resolution.

> The revelation from Jesus Christ, which God gave him to show His servants what must soon take place. He made it known by sending His angel to His servant John, who testifies to everything he saw—that is, the word of God and the testimony of Jesus Christ.
>
> Blessed is the one who reads aloud the words of this prophecy, and blessed are those who hear it and take to heart what is written in it, because the time is near.
> —**Revelation 1:1-3**
>
> I warn everyone who hears the words of the prophecy of this scroll: If anyone adds anything to them, God will add to that person the plagues described in this scroll.
>
> And if anyone takes words away from this scroll of prophecy, God will take away from that person any share in the tree of life and in the Holy City, which are described in this scroll. He who testifies to these things says, "Yes, I am coming soon." Amen. Come, Lord Jesus. The grace of the Lord Jesus be with God's people. Amen. —**Revelation 22:18-21**

The war started when astronomers observed explosions on the surface of Mars. Then, a meteor landed in England. The meteor turned out to be a mysterious metal cylinder.

One man approached the cylinder. He was immediately vaporized by a heat ray. Turns out the cylinder was an alien spaceship. Panic ensued.

The British military began to combat the spaceship. More cylinders began landing on Earth. The cylinders sprouted metallic tentacles and began striding around the countryside. They destroyed everything in their path. Helpless humans scrambled into hiding.

The struggle against Earthlings and Martians continued for weeks. When all hope seemed lost and the world was coming to an end, all the aliens suddenly died. One minute, chaos and destruction; the next minute, silence.

Turns out, the evil aliens died because of common diseases that our human bodies had become immune to. These microbes made the aliens sick to the point of death in a matter of weeks.[1] The earth was saved!

That's how H.G. Wells' famous *War of the Worlds* ends—with the terrifying aliens dropping dead without provocation. When an unsolvable problem is abruptly fixed for an implausible reason, it's called a *deux ex machina*. This phrase is Latin for "God from a machine."

*Deux ex machina* are used to end stories to reach a happy ending that may have seemed impossible. It a convenient way to end an inconvenient storytelling problem. In some cases, it's a cop-out.

The Bible ends with a slightly different Armageddon story. Its resolution involves God, but not one from a machine.

Revelation is the The End to the Bible. It details a vision revealed to the apostle John about the apocalypse.[2] Revelation involves symbolism and mysterious images. Perhaps more than any book in the Bible, it's the center of much misunderstanding and debate.

But one thing is certain about Revelation—it's the Bible's conclusion. It stands apart from all other books—they're historical, while Revelation is prophetic.

One of the reasons it's relevant to the biblical story is because it

---

1   Talk about germ warfare.
2   Except this version of the apocalypse doesn't involve an alien invasion.

involves the eventual return of Jesus. Many people refer to this as the Second Coming. It's believed that Jesus will come back to Earth, ending this age and escorting the righteous back to heaven. Talk about a dramatic ending to a story.

Regardless of your understanding of Revelation, it's no doubt a bold and curious way to end the Bible. The primary message is that the biblical story is not over. There are events which could happen in the future. It leaves the story open-ended so that we can find ourselves a part of God's narrative.

In most stories, this open-ended ending isn't usually satisfying. We want a conclusive ending that wraps up all loose ends and doesn't leave any lingering questions. The Bible is different because it's God's story and it's the truth.

Just as a story begins with a conflict, the story ends when that conflict is resolved. The biblical story begins with the introduction of sin and concludes when Jesus returns to wipe away our sins.

The fact that this resolution has not yet happened makes the biblical resolution very different from the end of most stories. God's story is not done.

## PRAYER

God, thank You for the book of Revelation because it means that Your story is not over. You've left the ending of the Bible up to our own interpretation and understanding.

We can read the Bible countless times, with new revelations and insights with each reading. Thank You for giving us such an incredible manuscript to connect with You. And help us to see our lives as a continuation of Your story. Amen.

## ACTION

Write the last paragraph of a story. It can be happy, tragic or some-where in between. Try to end it with something other than "And they lived happily ever after." Now imagine the story that's led to this point. How would you have gotten here if you'd written the entire thing?

## NOTES

And because no story is complete without one...

## THE END

# THE BIG IDEAS

Each of these Big Ideas is the perfect length to share on social media. Post quotes, storytelling examples and other thoughts using **#OriginalStoryteller** to join the conversation online. Share your story!

1. A story's **beginning** sets the tone for everything that's about to happen.

2. Storytelling is part of our DNA because we were modeled after the **Original Storyteller**—God.

3. **Words** are the basic building blocks of every story.

4. **Narratives** connect the elements of storytelling together into a recognizable pattern.

5. A **protagonist** gives a personality and focus to your story.

6. Effective **supporting characters** complement and amplify the actions of the story's protagonist.

7. **Antagonists** stand in the way of the protagonist, driving conflict in the story.

8. **Development** within a story's characters give them depth and authenticity.

9. Every story begins and ends within the framework of **conflict**.

10. **Actions** are the result of characters responding to conflict.

11. **Conversations** build relationships between characters and give a story credibility.

12. Every person and every story has a unique **perspective**.

13. A storyteller's **voice** is their own unique identity and ability to craft a story.

14. **Setting** establishes a story's context of both time and place.

15. A **motif** summarizes a story's main themes and ideas.

16. A character's **backstory** explains the motivation for their actions.

17. **Foreshadowing** builds anticipation for the story's coming action.

18. A **plot twist** relies on surprise to increase the impact of a story's climax.

19. An **author** has authority over a story, just has God as authority over creation.

20. Know your **audience** because who you're speaking to impacts what you say.

21. The more you build up to a story's **climax**, the greater the potential payoff.

22. The best stories are those that elicit great **emotion**.

23. **Suspension of disbelief** allows the audience to put aside their doubts while experiencing a story.

24. **Epistolaries** are more personal stories written in the form of letters.

25. **Universal truths** make a story relevant well beyond its original time and place.

26. Storytellers use **imagery** to paint a mental picture in the mind of the audience.

27. **Symbolism** transforms ordinary objects into the embodiment of complex concepts.

28. Many stories of heroes and adventure follow the same basic template called **The Hero's Journey**.

29. When **justice** becomes **poetic**, it means characters get what they deserve.

30. A story ends when the primary conflict comes to a **resolution**.

Be sure to visit www.OriginalStoryteller.com to learn more about the book, dowload exclusive content and buy more copies for your friends.

# ACKNOWLEDGMENTS

My sincerest gratitude to everyone who made this book possible.

To Justin Dean for your invaluable advice about writing a first book. To Kevin Hendricks and Mike Loomis for your honest feedback on my earliest drafts.

To Jonathan Malm for graciously contributing the forward. To Xavier Jones for designing the awesome cover.

To all of those who proofread this book when it was still in a terrible condition—especially David Clark and Jennifer Wilder, who gave it a much needed final revision.

To Jon Acuff for organizing the *30 Days of Hustle*, during which I wrote and edited the first draft. The program provided just the motivation and tips I needed to launch this project.

To everyone who read this book—even the acknowledgments section. A story is nothing without an audience. And you're an especially awesome one.

To my friends and family for supporting and encouraging me through this process. To my church small group for holding me accountable to finish this thing.

To my parents, Cady and Jerry, for reading books to me when I was younger. To my little sisters, Caroline and Rachel, for letting me read to them when they were younger.

Thanks especially to my wife, Victoria, for putting up with all of the time I've spent working on this book. And just for being the coolest all around person.

And thanks to God for writing the greatest story of all to serve as a divine inspiration for us all. It might sound cheesy, but it's true.

# ABOUT THE AUTHOR

**R**obert **Carnes** is a freelance writer and storyteller. He contributes to a number of blogs, including Orange Leaders, Church Marketing Sucks, ChurchMag, That Church Conference, Church.org and Sunday Mag.

Carnes has worked for a number of years in marketing and communications for both churches and nonprofits. He currently serves as a Managing Editor at the reThink Group in Atlanta, Ga., where he lives with his wife, Victoria.

Learn more by visiting www.jamrobcar.com or by following @jamrobcar on Twitter and Instagram.